SHOPPING GUIDE FOR

CARING
CONSUMERS

A GUIDE TO PRODUCTS THAT ARE NOT TESTED ON ANIMALS

PEOPLE FOR THE ETHICAL TREATMENT OF ANIMALS

PETA attempts to update this guide annually. However, we may not receive a company's updated information before going to print. Therefore, this guide is based on the most current information available at the time of printing. Companies not listed as cruelty-free may be cruelty-free but are not included because they have not sent PETA a letter stating their complete rejection of animal testing, nor signed PETA's statement of assurance, nor signed the Corporate Standard of Compassion for Animals (CSCA). Companies identified as conducting animal tests may have changed their animal-testing policies after this edition went to print. Inclusion on any list is not an endorsement by PETA of any company and/or its products. For periodically updated company information, please contact PETA.

PETA's updated *2001 Shopping Guide for Caring Consumers* lists more than 550 cruelty-free cosmetics, household, and personal-care product companies, making it easy to find everything from hair color and furniture polish to correction fluid and more.

© 2000 PETA   ISBN# 1-57067-106-0

People for the Ethical Treatment of Animals
501 Front St.
Norfolk, VA 23510

Edited by Ann Marie D. Giunti
Proofread by Karen Martino and Karen Porreca
Designed by Meg Caskey

TABLE OF CONTENTS

This guide, now in its 11th edition, started out as a fold-out, wallet-sized pamphlet listing a handful of companies that didn't test their products on animals. You can see for yourself how the growing public concern with animal suffering has translated into real results: Our list of cruelty-free companies has grown to include more than 550 companies, including The Body Shop, Mary Kay, Estée Lauder, and Revlon, that have signed PETA's statement of assurance or the Corporate Standard of Compassion for Animals. They've put their commitment in writing, guaranteeing that they do not (and never will) test ingredients or finished products on animals.

The list of vegan companies (those that use alternatives to both animal testing and animal ingredients) has grown, too. Many of these companies proudly advertise on their labels that they use no lanolin, beeswax, or other animal ingredients—and with our list, it's easier than ever for you to buy only vegan cosmetics and household products. Also, to help you find stylish, comfortable alternatives to leather shoes, belts, handbags, and other accessories, this guide includes "Alternatives to Leather and Other Animal Products." It's a cinch to take the "moo" out of your shoes!

Our "Health Charities" list is included to help you decide which charities deserve your support. Many compassionate people refuse to support charities that blind, burn, mutilate, or otherwise use and kill animals in cruel animal experiments. On this list, you'll find many caring charities that help people without hurting animals.

Be proud of your efforts to make this a kinder world for animals. The care you take in seeking out a cruelty-free lipstick or laundry detergent makes a strong statement—that you refuse to participate in the killing of animals in Draize eye, skin irritancy, and lethal dose tests. Caring consumers like you are helping to ensure that more companies will abandon animal tests, choosing instead to use effective, humane alternatives such as tissue and cell cultures and computer models. As the demand for cruelty-free products grows, so will their availability. Again, thanks for your concern and respect for animals and your commitment to cruelty-free living.

WHAT WOULD YOU DO TO SAVE AN ANIMAL?

Rue McClanahan

Animals have long held a special place in my heart—their companionship has always been very important to me. That's why it distresses me to tell you that tens of thousands of animals are suffering needlessly.

They desperately need help—and organizations like PETA.

Since 1980, People for the Ethical Treatment of Animals has become this nation's most effective advocate in behalf of animal protection. The people at PETA are committed to exposing and stopping animal cruelty—especially in laboratories.

It feels great to use my voice for animals. Please join me, and contact PETA today. You can help save animals, too.

For more information on how you can become part of this vital work, write PETA, 501 Front St., Norfolk, VA 23510, or call 757-622-PETA.

Rue

PeTA

THE SHOPPING GUIDE FOR CARING CONSUMERS

People for the Ethical Treatment of Animals (PETA) has compiled this 11th edition of the *Shopping Guide for Caring Consumers* as a part of our international Caring Consumer Project. It's an easy resource to use when shopping for products made by companies that do not test on animals.

The companies listed in this guide have signed PETA's statement of assurance or provided a company policy statement verifying that they:

• Do not conduct animal tests on ingredients or finished products

• Do not contract with other laboratories to conduct animal tests

• Will not conduct animal tests in the future

Some companies listed have signed the Corporate Standard of Compassion for Animals (see page 8), which, in addition to verifying compliance with the three requirements above, also requires companies to obtain statements of assurance from all their suppliers to the effect that no ingredients supplied to them were tested on animals.

WHAT IS THE "CORPORATE STANDARD OF COMPASSION FOR ANIMALS"?

The Coalition for Consumer Information on Cosmetics (CCIC) joins together PETA and six other animal protection groups that have created a unified policy designed to make it easier for consumers to identify the products that meet ethical standards. The Corporate Standard of Compassion for Animals (CSCA) is that unified policy, and PETA is encouraging all companies, including those that have signed PETA's statement of assurance, to adopt the CSCA. For more details about the CCIC or the CSCA, call 1-888-546-CCIC or check out www.LeapingBunny.org.

BLINDING BUNNIES AND POISONING MICE: OUTDATED, UNNECESSARY, AND CRUEL

Every year, millions of rabbits, mice, rats, guinea pigs, and other animals suffer and are killed in painful product tests. Companies claim to use these outdated tests to determine the safety of cosmetics, household, and other consumer products.

However, these tests are widely criticized by scientists as being cruel, archaic methods that offer unreliable and often contradictory results. Furthermore, the Food and Drug Administration (FDA) and the Consumer Product Safety Commission do not require the use of animals to test cosmetics or household products.

The notoriously cruel and unnecessary lethal dose tests and the Draize eye irritancy tests, which are still used today, date back to the 1920s. In lethal dose tests, animals are force-fed, injected with, or forced to inhale toxic substances until a designated percentage of them die. In the Draize eye irritancy tests, a substance is smeared into the eyes of albino rabbits, usually without anesthesia. The rabbits are restrained, their eyelids held open with clips, and they are forced to endure these conditions for up to 18 days. They suffer inflammation, ulceration, hemorrhage, and blindness.

Modern technology has enabled hundreds of companies to use non-animal test methods, including human volunteers as test subjects, *in vitro* studies, computer models, cloned human skin, tissue cultures, and extensive databases. These sophisticated, reliable, humane alternatives are helping to ensure that cruel product tests on animals will soon be a shameful page in our history books.

"V" IS FOR VEGAN

Skin lotion, shaving cream, toothpaste, and lipstick—many of these cosmetics and personal care products contain slaughterhouse byproducts. They may also contain other animal-derived ingredients, including honey, silk and silk byproducts, lanolin, and substances extracted from insects or sea animals.

Many consumers who refuse to support industries in which animal suffering is inherent seek out vegan products. PETA lists products as vegan when they are free of any animal products, including slaughterhouse byproducts. Vegan products listed in this guide may contain plant- or mineral-based or synthetic ingredients. Companies listed in this guide that are marked with a ♥ manufacture only vegan products.

Sometimes labels include ingredients that can be of either vegetable or animal origin, including cetyl alcohol, glycerin, lecithin, mono- and diglycerides, stearic acid, and squalene. When in doubt, contact the manufacturer for details. Please note that most companies on our "don't test" list make at least some vegan products. Please check with the companies for more information about these products.

For a list of common animal ingredients and their alternatives, please see page 97.

LOOK FOR THE NEW LOGO

As part of our involvement with the Coalition for Consumer Information on Cosmetics (CCIC), PETA's Caring Consumer Product Logo has been replaced by CCIC's new logo. When you see this logo, you can be sure that the product meets the non-animal testing standards of the Corporate Standard of Compassion for Animals (CSCA).

For more information about product testing or other animal rights issues, please contact:

People for the Ethical Treatment of Animals (PETA)
501 Front St.
Norfolk, VA 23510
757-622-PETA
www.peta-online.org

COMPANIES THAT DON'T TEST ON ANIMALS

What Types of Companies Are on the "Don't Test" List?

The list includes cosmetics, personal care, household cleaning, and office supply companies only. PETA's Caring Consumer Project was founded upon the principle that no law requires animal testing of these types of products, so manufacturers of these products have no excuse for animal testing and should be boycotted in order to pressure them to change to a non-animal testing policy.

This list does not include companies that manufacture only products that are required by law to be tested on animals (e.g., pharmaceuticals, automotive and garden chemicals, food additives, etc.). While PETA is opposed to all animal testing, our quarrel in this matter is with the regulatory agencies that require animal testing. Nonetheless, it is important to let companies know that it is their responsibility to convince the regulatory agencies that there is a better way to determine product safety.

The "don't test" list may include companies that manufacture both products that are and products that are not required to be tested on animals, but in order to be listed, each company has stated that it does not conduct any animal tests that are not required by law.

LEGEND

- ♥ Vegan. (Companies that manufacture strictly vegan products, i.e., containing no animal products. Companies without this symbol may still offer some vegan products.)

- ★ Company meets Corporate Standard of Compassion for Animals (CSCA).

- ✇ Company using Coalition for Consumer Information on Cosmetics (CCIC) logo. (All companies listed in the guide are cruelty-free. Many of them have chosen to use a logo to assist consumers.)

- ⊠ Mail order available.

- 🛒 Companies' products can be purchased through the PETA Mall at www.PETAMall.com. PETA will receive a percentage of every purchase.

ABBA Products
7400 E. Tierra Buena
Scottsdale, AZ 85260
480-609-6000
800-848-4475
www.styl.com
Products: dandruff
shampoo, hair care,
permanents
Availability: boutiques,
distributors, salons,
specialty stores
♥

ABEnterprises
425 A Myrtle Greens Dr.
Conway, SC 29526
843-234-0740
Products: aromatherapy,
bathing supply, dental
hygiene, deodorant, hair
care, herbal supplements,
household supply, shaving
supply, skin care, soap,
vitamins
Availability: mail order
✉

Abercrombie & Fitch
4 Limited Pkwy.
Reynoldsburg, OH 43068
614-577-6570
Products: fragrance for men,
personal care, toiletries
Availability: Abercrombie &
Fitch stores, Victoria's
Secret stores

Abkit
207 E. 94th St., Ste. 201
New York, NY 10128
212-860-8358
800-CAMOCARE
Products: hair care, skin
care
Availability: health food
stores, mail order
✉

Abra Therapeutics
10365 Hwy. 116
Forestville, CA 95436
707-869-0761
800-745-0761
www.abratherapeutics.com
Products: aromatherapy,
baby care, bathing supply,
herbal supplements, hypo-
allergenic skin care for men
and women, shaving
supply, sun care, toiletries,
vitamins
Availability: boutiques,
health food stores, mail
order, spas, specialty stores
♥ ✉

Advanage Wonder Cleaner
16615 S. Halsted St.
Harvey, IL 60426
708-333-7644
800-323-6444
www.wondercleaner.com
Products: carpet cleaning
supply, fine washables
detergent, laundry
detergent, oven cleaner
Availability: independent
sales representatives, mail
order
♥ ✉

Ahimsa Natural Care
1250 Reid St., Ste. 13A
Richmond Hill, ON L4B
1G3
Canada
905-709-8977
888-424-4672
Products: aromatherapy,
baby care, dandruff
shampoo, fragrance for men
and women, hair care
Availability: boutiques,
cooperatives,
environmentally friendly
stores, health food stores,
mail order, specialty stores
♥ ✉

Alba Botanica
1105 Industrial Ave.
Petaluma, CA 94952
707-769-5120
www.albabotanica.com
Products: bathing supply,
shaving supply, skin care for
men and women, soap, sun
care, toiletries
Availability: boutiques,
cooperatives, drugstores,
health food stores, mail
order, specialty stores
★ ✉

**Alexandra Avery Body
Botanicals**
4717 S.E. Belmont
Portland, OR 97215
503-236-5926
800-669-1863
Products: aromatherapy,
fragrance for men and
women, lubricants, shaving
supply, skin care, soap, sun
care, toiletries
Availability: boutiques,
cooperatives, health food
stores, mail order, specialty
stores
✉

**Alexandra de Markoff
(Parlux)**
3725 S.W. 30th Ave.
Ft. Lauderdale, FL 33312
954-316-9008
800-727-5895
Products: cosmetics
Availability: department
stores

Allens Naturally
P.O. Box 514, Dept. M
Farmington, MI 48332-0514
734-453-5410
800-352-8971
www.allensnaturally.com
Products: fruit and
vegetable wash, household
supply, laundry detergent
Availability: cooperatives,
health food stores, mail
order
♥ ★ ✉

Almay (Revlon)
625 Madison Ave.
New York, NY 10022
212-572-5000
Products: cosmetics,
deodorant, ethnic personal
care, hypo-allergenic skin
care for men and women,
sun care
Availability: department
stores, drugstores,
supermarkets

Aloegen Natural Cosmetics
9200 Mason Ave.
Chatsworth, CA 91311
818-882-2951
800-327-2012
www.levlad.com
Products: skin care
Availability: cooperatives,
health food stores, mail
order
✉

Aloette Cosmetics
1301 Wright's Ln. E.
West Chester, PA 19380
610-692-0600
800-ALOETTE
Products: bathing supply,
cosmetics, fragrance for
men and women, nail care,
skin care for men and
women, sun care, toiletries
Availability: independent
sales representatives

Aloe Up
P.O. Box 831
6908 W. Expressway 83
Harlingen, TX 78551
210-428-0081
800-537-2563
Products: hair care, hypo-
allergenic skin care for men
and women, sun care,
toiletries
Availability: boutiques,
drugstores, health food
stores, mail order, specialty
stores, supermarkets
✉

Aloe Vera of America
9660 Dilworth Rd.
Dallas, TX 75243
214-343-5700
Products: aromatherapy,
bathing supply, companion
animal care, cosmetics,
dental hygiene, deodorant,
hair care, household supply,
laundry detergent, shaving
supply, skin care, soap,
vitamins
Availability: independent
sales representatives

Alvin Last
425 Sawmill River Rd.
Ardsley, NY 10502
914-376-1000
800-527-8123
www.alast.com
Products: cosmetics,
dandruff shampoo, dental
hygiene, hair care, hair
color (henna), shaving
supply, skin care for men
and women, toiletries
Availability: drugstores,
health food stores, mail
order
✉

Amazon Premium Products
P.O. Box 530156
Miami, FL 33153
305-757-1943
800-832-5645
www.amazonpp.com
Products: air freshener,
carpet cleaning supply,
furniture polish
Availability: hardware
stores, mail order
♥ ✉

American Formulating & Manufacturing
3251 Third Ave.
San Diego, CA 92103
619-239-0321
800-239-0321
www.afmsafecoat.com
Products: carpet cleaning
supply, floor finishes, hair
care, household supply,
paint, stain
Availability: cooperatives,
mail order, specialty stores
♥ ★ ✉

American International
2220 Gaspar Ave.
Los Angeles, CA 90040
213-728-2999
Products: skin care,
toiletries
Availability: beauty supply
stores, boutiques, discount
department stores,
drugstores, health food
stores, specialty stores,
supermarkets

13

American Safety Razor
1 Razor Blade Ln.
Verona, VA 24482
540-248-8000
800-445-9284
Products: aromatherapy,
bathing supply, Bump
Fighter, Burma Shave,
Flicker, Gem, Personna,
razors, shaving supply,
soap, toiletries
Availability: boutiques,
department stores, discount
department stores,
drugstores, health food
stores, mail order, specialty
stores, supermarkets
⊠

**America's Finest Products
Corporation**
1639 Ninth St.
Santa Monica, CA 90404
310-450-6555
800-482-6555
Products: all-purpose
cleaning supply, concrete
cleaner, Elbow Grease, fine
washables detergent,
household supply, laundry
soil-stain remover, liquid
cleaner, water softener
Availability: drugstores, mail
order, supermarkets
♥ ⊠

**Amitée Cosmetics
(Advanced Research Labs)**
151 Kalmus Dr., Ste. H3
Costa Mesa, CA 92626
714-556-1028
800-966-6960
Products: hair care
Availability: beauty supply
stores, drugstores,
supermarkets

Amoresse Laboratories
3435 Wilshire Blvd., #975
Los Angeles, CA 90010
800-258-7931
Products: nail care
Availability: salons

Amway Corporation
7575 E. Fulton Rd.
Ada, MI 49355-0001
616-787-4278
www.amway.com
Products: car care, carpet
cleaning supply, cosmetics,
dandruff shampoo, dental
hygiene, fragrance, furniture
polish, hair care, insect
repellent, laundry detergent,
oven cleaner, skin care, sun
care, vitamins
Availability: independent
sales representatives, mail
order
⊠

Ancient Formulas
638 W. 33rd St. N.
Wichita, KS 67204
316-838-5600
800-543-3026
Products: acne care,
carbohydrate balance,
dental hygiene, hypo-
allergenic and herbal
supplements for blood
pressure, irregularity,
prostate health, respiratory
health, sleeping aid
Availability: cooperatives,
drugstores, health food
stores, mail order,
physicians
⊠

**Andrea International
Industries**
2220 Gaspar Ave.
Los Angeles, CA 90040
213-728-2999
Products: nail care, skin
care for women
Availability: boutiques,
discount department stores,
drugstores, mass retailers,
specialty stores,
supermarkets

The Apothecary Shoppe
P.O. Box 57
Lake Oswego, OR 97034
503-635-6652
800-487-8839
www.herbed.com
Products: aromatherapy,
flower essences, herbal
supplements,
homeobotanicals, iridology
supply
Availability: mail order,
Web site
⊠

Aramis (Estée Lauder)
767 Fifth Ave.
New York, NY 10153
212-572-3700
Products: bathing supply,
deodorant, fragrance for
men and women, hair care,
razors, shaving supply, skin
care for men and women,
soap, sun care, toiletries
Availability: department
stores, specialty stores

Arbonne International
15 Argonaut
Aliso Viejo, CA 92656
949-770-2610
800-ARBONNE
Products: bathing supply,
cosmetics, fragrance for
women, hair care, herbal
supplements, hypo-
allergenic skin care for men
and women, nutritional bars
and shakes (not vegan),
shaving supply, sun care,
vitamins
Availability: independent
sales representatives

★ ☟

Ardell International
2220 Gaspar Ave.
Los Angeles, CA 90040
213-728-2999
Products: nail care, skin
care for women
Availability: boutiques,
discount department stores,
drugstores, mass retailers,
specialty stores,
supermarkets

Arizona Natural Resources
2525 E. Beardsley Rd.
Phoenix, AZ 85050
602-569-6900
Products: aromatherapy,
bathing supply, deodorant,
hair care, skin care, sun
care
Availability: department
stores, drug stores, health
food stores, supermarkets

Aromaland
1326 Rufina Cir.
Santa Fe, NM 87505
505-438-0402
800-933-5267
www.buyaromatherapy.com
Products: aromatherapy,
bathing supply, educational
materials, fragrance, insect
repellent, nail care, natural
body care, skin care, soap
Availability: bookstores,
health food stores, salons,
spas, Web site

✉

Aroma Vera
5901 Rodeo Rd.
Los Angeles, CA 90016-
4312
310-280-0407
800-669-9514
www.aromavera.com
Products: air freshener,
aromatherapy, bathing
supply, fragrance for men
and women, hair care, skin
care for men and women,
soap, toiletries
Availability: Aroma Vera
stores, boutiques, health
food stores, mail order,
salons, spas, specialty stores

✉

Astonish Industries, Inc.
Commerce Lane
Business Pk.
423 Commerce Ln., Unit 2
West Berlin, NJ 08091
609-753-7078
800-530-5385
Products: carpet cleaning
supply, dish detergent,
household supply, oven
cleaner
Availability: mail order,
QVC, specialty stores

♥ ✉

Atmosa Brand
Aromatherapy Products
1420 Fifth Ave., Ste. 2200
Seattle, WA 98101-2378
206-521-5986
Products: aromatherapy,
home fragrance
Availability: boutiques,
department stores, specialty
stores

♥

Aubrey Organics, Inc.
4419 N. Manhattan Ave.
Tampa, FL 33614
813-877-4186
800-AUBREYH
www.aubrey-organics.com
Products: baby care,
bathing supply, companion
animal care, cosmetics,
deodorant, fragrance for
men and women, hair care,
hair color, household
supply, insect repellent,
shaving supply, skin care,
sun care
Availability: health food
stores, Web site

✉

Aunt Bee's Skin Care
P.O. Box 2678
Rancho de Taos, NM 87577
505-737-0522
888-233-2256
Products: aromatherapy, lip
balm, skin care, soap, sun
care
Availability: drugstores,
health food stores,
supermarkets

Aura Cacia
P.O. Box 311
Norway, IA 52318
800-437-3301
www.auracacia.com
Products: aromatherapy, baby care, bathing supply, fragrance for men and women, skin care, soap, toiletries
Availability: boutiques, cooperatives, discount department stores, drugstores, health food stores, mail order, specialty stores
✉

Auromère Ayurvedic Imports
2621 W. Hwy. 12
Lodi, CA 95242
209-339-3710
www.auromere.com
Products: ayurvedic supply, bathing supply, dental hygiene, herbal supplements, incense, massage oil, skin care for men and women, soap, toiletries, vitamins
Availability: health food stores, New Age bookstores
♥ ★ ✉

The Australasian College of Herbal Studies
530 First St., Ste. A
P.O. Box 57
Lake Oswego, OR 97034
503-635-6652
800-487-8839
www.herbed.com
Products: aromatherapy, correspondence courses in natural healing, herbal supplements
Availability: mail order, Web site
✉

Autumn-Harp
61 Pine St.
Bristol, VT 05443
802-453-4807
Products: aromatherapy, baby care, cosmetics, nonprescription therapy, personal care, sun care
Availability: cooperatives, department stores, drugstores, health food stores, mail order, supermarkets
★ ✉

Avalon Organic Botanicals
1105 Industrial Ave.
Petaluma, CA 94952
707-769-5120
www.avalonproducts.net
Products: bathing supply, deodorant, hair care, hypo-allergenic skin care for men and women, soap, toiletries
Availability: boutiques, health food stores, mail order, specialty stores
♥ ★ ✉

**Aveda Corporation
(Estée Lauder)**
4000 Pheasant Ridge Dr.
Blaine, MN 55449
612-783-4000
800-328-0849
www.aveda.com
Products: cosmetics, ethnic personal care, hair care, lifestyle items, Pure-fume (R), skin care
Availability: educational institutions, environmentally friendly stores, health care facilities, salons, spas

Avigal Henna
45-49 Davis St.
Long Island City, NY 11101
718-361-3123
800-722-1011
Products: henna hair color
Availability: health food stores, salons, specialty stores
♥

Avon
1251 Ave. of the Americas
New York, NY 10020
212-546-6015
800-858-8000
www.avon.com
Products: cosmetics, dandruff shampoo, ethnic personal care, fragrance for men and women, hair care, hypo-allergenic skin care for men and women, nail care, Skin-So-Soft insect repellent, sun care, toiletries
Availability: distributors, mail order
✉ ⌷

Ayurherbal Corporation
1100 Lotus Dr.
Silver Lake, WI 53170
414-889-8569
Products: air freshener, dental hygiene, fragrance for men and women, household supply, incense, toiletries
Availability: boutiques, cooperatives, drugstores, health food stores, mail order, specialty stores
♥ ✉

Ayurveda Holistic Center
82A Bayville Ave.
Bayville, NY 11709
516-628-8200
www.ayurveda.com
Products: ayurvedic herbs for humans and companion animals
Availability: Ayurveda Holistic Center stores, health food stores
♥

Bare Escentuals
600 Townsend St.
Ste. 329-E
San Francisco, CA 94103
415-487-3400
800-227-3990
Products: aromatherapy, bathing supply, cosmetics, deodorant, fragrance, hair care, hypo-allergenic skin care, nail care, shaving supply, soap, toiletries
Availability: Bare Escentuals stores, boutiques, department stores, mail order, specialty stores
✉

Basically Natural
109 E. G St.
Brunswick, MD 21716
301-834-7923
800-352-7099
Products: air freshener, aromatherapy, baby care, bleach, car care, companion animal care, cosmetics, dental hygiene, hair care, insect repellent, laundry detergent, oven cleaner, skin care, sun care
Availability: mail order
♥ ✉

Basic Elements Hair Care System
28364 Southwestern Ave. #487
Rancho Palos Verdes, CA 90275
800-947-5522
Products: hair care, skin care for men and women
Availability: mail order, salons
♥ ⊠

Basis (Beiersdorf)
BDF Plz.
360 Martin Luther King Dr.
Norwalk, CT 06856-5529
203-853-8008
Products: soap
Availability: drugstores, supermarkets

Bath & Body Works
7 Limited Pkwy. E.
Reynoldsburg, OH 43068
614-856-6585
800-395-1001
Products: air freshener, aromatherapy, baby care, bathing supply, cosmetics, deodorant, fragrance, hair care, hypo-allergenic skin care, insect repellent, nail care, shaving supply, soap, sun care
Availability: Bath & Body Works stores

Bath Island
469 Amsterdam Ave.
New York, NY 10024
212-787-9415
www.bathisland.com
Products: air freshener, aromatherapy, baby care, bathing supply, dandruff shampoo, dental hygiene, deodorant, fragrance, hair care, household supply, nail care, razors, skin care, soap, sun care, toothbrushes
Availability: Bath Island store, mail order
⊠

Baudelaire
170 Emerald St.
Keene, NH 03431
603-352-9234
800-327-2324
www.baudelairesoaps.com
Products: aromatherapy, baby care, bathing supply, fragrance for men and women, shaving supply, skin care, soap, toiletries
Availability: bed and bath stores, drugstores, gift boutiques, health food stores
★ ⊠

BeautiControl Cosmetics
2121 Midway Rd.
Carrollton, TX 75006
972-458-0601
www.beauticontrol.com
Products: cosmetics, fragrance for men and women, hypo-allergenic skin care, nail care, sun care
Availability: distributors

Beauty Naturally
P.O. Box 4905
850 Stanton Rd.
Burlingame, CA 94010
650-697-1845
800-432-4323
www.beautynaturally.com
Products: dandruff shampoo, deodorant, hair care, hair color, hypo-allergenic skin care for men and women, permanents
Availability: health food stores, mail order
⊠

Beauty Without Cruelty
1105 Industrial Ave.
Petaluma, CA 94952
707-769-5120
www.avalonproducts.net
Products: aromatherapy, bathing supply, cosmetics, hair care, hypo-allergenic skin care for men and women, nail care, soap, sun care, toiletries
Availability: boutiques, health food stores, mail order, specialty stores
♥ ★ ⊠

Beehive Botanicals
16297 W. Nursery Rd.
Hayward, WI 54843-7138
715-634-4274
800-233-4483
www.beehive-botanicals.com
Products: bathing supply, dental hygiene, hair care, herbal supplements, skin care for women, soap, toiletries
Availability: health food stores, mail order
⊠

Beiersdorf
BDF Plz.
360 Martin Luther King Dr.
Norwalk, CT 06856-5529
203-853-8008
Products: Basis soap,
Eucerin, La Prairie, Nivea,
skin care
Availability: drugstores,
supermarkets

Bella's Secret Garden
P.O. Box 3994
Westlake, CA 91359
805-373-0040
www.bellassecretgarden.com
Products: air freshener, baby
care, fragrance for women,
hair care, household supply,
hypo-allergenic skin care
for men and women,
toiletries
Availability: boutiques,
department stores,
drugstores

Belle Star
23151 Alcalde, #A1
Laguna Hills, CA 92653
714-768-7006
800-442-STAR
Products: aromatherapy,
fragrance for men and
women, incense, toiletries
Availability: Belle Star store,
boutiques, craft shows, mail
order, specialty stores
✉

Berol (Sanford)
2711 Washington Blvd.
Bellwood, IL 60104
708-547-5525
800-438-3703
www.sanfordcorp.com
Products: ink, office supply,
writing instruments
Availability: department
stores, drugstores, mail
order, office supply stores,
supermarkets
✉

Better Botanicals
335 Victory Dr.
Herndon, VA 20170
202-625-6815
888-BB-HERBS
www.betterbotanicals.com
Products: aromatherapy,
ayurvedic hair care,
ayurvedic skin care for men
and women, baby care,
bathing supply, soap
Availability: boutiques,
health food stores, Internet,
spas
★ ✉

Beverly Hills Cold Wax
P.O. Box 600476
San Diego, CA 92160
619-283-0880
800-833-0889
Products: cold wax natural
hair remover
Availability: beauty supply
stores, health food stores,
mail order, salons
✉

BioFilm
3121 Scott St.
Vista, CA 92083
619-727-9030
800-848-5900
Products: Astroglide
personal lubricant
Availability: drugstores
♥

Biogime International, Inc.
25602 I-45 N., Ste. 106
Spring, TX 77386
281-298-2607
800-338-8784
www.biogimeskincare.com
Products: bathing supply,
cosmetics, hypo-allergenic
skin care for men and
women, lotions, sun care,
theatrical makeup
Availability: independent
sales representatives, mail
order
♥ ✉

Biokosma (Caswell-Massey)
100 Enterprise Pl.
Dover, DE 19904
800-326-0500
www.caswell-massey.com
Products: toiletries
Availability: mail order,
specialty stores
✉

Bio Pac
584 Pinto Ct.
Incline Village, NV 89451
800-225-2855
www.bio-pac.com
Products: dish detergent,
hair care, household
cleansers, laundry
detergent, nonchlorine
bleach, soap
Availability: health food
stores
♥ ★ ✉

Bio-Tec Cosmetics
630 Mount Pleasant Rd.
2nd Fl.
Toronto, ON M4S2N1
Canada
416-483-6300
800-667-2524
Products: cosmetics, hair
care, hair color,
permanents, skin care for
men and women, toiletries
Availability: bath and skin
care in retail outlets, hair
care in beauty salons

Biotone
4757 Old Cliffs Rd.
San Diego, CA 92120
619-582-0027
Products: aromatherapy,
massage creams, oil and
lotion for massage therapists
Availability: boutiques,
direct to massage therapists,
independent sales
representatives, mail order,
specialty stores
⊠

Bobbi Brown (Estée Lauder)
767 Fifth Ave.
New York, NY 10153
212-572-4200
Products: cosmetics, ethnic
personal care
Availability: department
stores

**Bo-Chem Company
(Neway)**
42 Doaks Ln.
Marblehead, MA 01945
617-631-9400
Products: household supply
Availability: distributors,
mail order
⊠

Body Encounters
604 Manor Rd.
Cinnaminson, NJ 08077
800-839-2639
www.bodyencounters.com
Products: aromatherapy,
bathing supply, skin care for
men and women, soap, sun
care, toiletries
Availability: mail order,
Web site
⊠

Bodyography
1641 16th St.
Santa Monica, CA 90404
310-399-2886
800-642-2639
Products: cosmetics
Availability: beauty supply
stores, salons

The Body Shop
5036 One World Way
Wake Forest, NC 27587
919-554-4900
800-541-2535
www.the-body-shop.com
Products: aromatherapy,
baby care, bathing supply,
cosmetics, dental hygiene,
deodorant, fragrance, hair
care, hair color, nail care,
razors, shaving supply, skin
care, soap, sun care,
toiletries, toothbrushes
Availability: mail order, The
Body Shop stores
★ ⊠

Body Time
1101 Eighth St., Ste. 100
Berkeley, CA 94710
510-524-0216
888-649-2639
www.bodytime.com
Products: aromatherapy,
baby care, bathing supply,
essential oil, hair care,
shaving supply, skin care for
men and women, sun care,
toiletries
Availability: Body Time
stores, mail order
⊠

Bon Ami/Faultless Starch
510 Walnut St.
Kansas City, MO 64106-
1209
816-842-1230
Products: household supply
Availability: cooperatives,
drugstores, health food
stores, supermarkets

Bonne Bell
1006 Crocker Rd.
Westlake, OH 44145
440-808-2410
www.bonnebell.com
Products: bathing supply,
cosmetics, nail care, skin
care for women, soap, sun
care, toiletries
Availability: department
stores, drugstores,
supermarkets
⊠

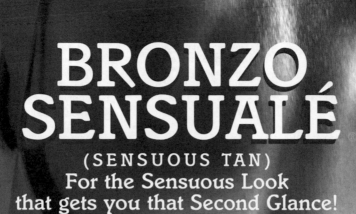

Börlind of Germany
P.O. Box 130
New London, NH 03257-0130
603-526-2076
800-447-7024
www.borlind.com
Products: aromatherapy, cosmetics, hair care, toiletries
Availability: boutiques, health food stores, salons, spas, specialty stores
★ ✉

Botan Corporation
2620 Drayton Dr.
Louisville, KY 40205-2332
502-454-3503
Products: hypo-allergenic skin care for men and women, shaving supply, toiletries
Availability: department stores, distributors, drugstores, environmentally friendly bath stores, health food stores, mail order, specialty stores
♥ ✉

Botanics Skin Care
P.O. Box 384
Ukiah, CA 95482
707-462-6141
800-800-6141
Products: hair care, hypo-allergenic skin care, sun care
Availability: boutiques, cooperatives, department stores, health food stores, mail order, specialty stores
✉

Brocato International
1 Main St., Ste. 501
Minneapolis, MN 55414
800-243-0275
Products: dandruff shampoo, hair care, permanents
Availability: boutiques, salons, specialty stores
♥

Bronzo Sensualé
1020 Stillwater Dr.
Miami Beach, FL 33141
305-867-1744
800-991-2226
www.bronzosensuale.com
Products: aromatherapy, baby care, condoms/lubricants, hypo-allergenic skin care for men and women, sun care
Availability: boutiques, drugstores, health food stores, mail order, resorts, spas, specialty stores
♥ ★ ✉

Brookside Soap Company
P.O. Box 55638
Seattle, WA 98155
425-742-2265
Products: soap
Availability: health food stores
♥

Bug Off
197 N. Willard St.
Burlington, VT 05401
802-865-6290
Products: herbal insect repellent for home, people, and companion animals
Availability: cooperatives, environmentally friendly stores, health food stores, mail order, sporting goods stores, veterinarians
♥ ✉

Caeran
280 King George Rd.
Brantford, ON N3R 5L6
Canada
519-751-0513
800-563-2974
Products: baby care, car care, carpet cleaning supply, companion animal care, dandruff shampoo, hair care, household supply, hypo-allergenic skin care, laundry detergent, sun care, toiletries, vitamins
Availability: boutiques, health food stores, independent sales representatives, mail order, specialty stores
✉

California Styles
5823 Newton Dr.
Carlsbad, CA 92008
800-LA-COSTA
Products: cosmetics, hair care, nail care, shaving supply, skin care for women, sun care, toiletries
Availability: mail order, salons
✉

California SunCare
10877 Wilshire Blvd.
12th Fl.
Los Angeles, CA 90024
800-SUN-CARE
Products: self-tanning products, skin care for men and women
Availability: salons

CamoCare Camomile Skin Care Products
207 E. 94th St., Ste. 201
New York, NY 10128
212-860-8358
800-CAMOCARE
www.abkit.com
Products: hair care, skin care
Availability: health food stores, mail order
⊠

Candy Kisses Natural Lip Balm
16 E. 40th St., 12th Fl.
New York, NY 10016
212-951-3035
www.candykisses.com
Products: cosmetics
Availability: discount department stores, drugstores, mail order, supermarkets
♥ ★ ⊠

Carina Supply
464 Granville St.
Vancouver, BC V6C 1V4
Canada
604-687-3617
Products: companion animal care, dandruff shampoo, hair care, hair color, hypo-allergenic skin care for men and women, permanents
Availability: Carina Supply stores, companion animal supply stores, groomers, mail order, salons, veterinarians
⊠

Carlson Laboratories
15 College Dr.
Arlington Heights, IL 60004
847-255-1600
800-323-4141
Products: hair care, personal care, skin care, toiletries, vitamins
Availability: health food stores

Carma Laboratories
5801 W. Airways Ave.
Franklin, WI 53132
414-421-7707
www.carma-labs.com
Products: Carmex lip balm/cold sore medicine, nonprescription therapy, personal care
Availability: department stores, drugstores, health food stores, supermarkets
⊠

Caswell-Massey
121 Fieldcrest Ave.
Edison, NJ 08818
201-225-2181
800-326-0500
www.caswellmasseyltd.com
Products: aromatherapy, baby care, bathing supply, dental hygiene, deodorant, fragrance, hair care, shaving supply, skin care, soap, toiletries, toothbrushes
Availability: boutiques, Caswell-Massey stores, department stores, discount department stores, drugstores, health food stores, mail order, specialty stores
⊠

Celestial Body, Inc.
21298 Pleasant Hill Rd.
Boonville, MO 65233
660-882-6858
800-882-6858
Products: aromatherapy, bathing supply, feminine hygiene, hypo-allergenic skin care for men and women, shaving supply, soap, toiletries
Availability: boutiques, cooperatives, health food stores, independent sales representatives, mail order, specialty stores
⊠

Chanel
9 W. 57th St.
New York, NY 10019
212-688-5055
Products: cosmetics, deodorant, fragrance for men and women, nail care, skin care for men and women, soap, sun care, toiletries
Availability: Chanel stores, department stores

Chatoyant Pearl Cosmetics
P.O. Box 526
Port Townsend, WA 98368
206-385-4825
Products: skin care, toiletries
Availability: health food stores

Christian Dior Perfumes
9 W. 57th St.
New York, NY 10019
212-759-1840
Products: cosmetics, fragrance for men and women, nail care, skin care, toiletries
Availability: boutiques, department stores, specialty stores

Christine Valmy, Inc.
285 Change Bridge Rd.
Pine Brook, NJ 07058
973-575-1050
800-526-5057
Products: aromatherapy,
bathing supply, skin care,
soap, sun care
Availability: independent
distributors, salons
⊠

Chuckles (Farmavita)
P.O. Box 5126
Manchester, NH 03109
603-669-4228
800-221-3496
www.sukesha.com
Products: hair care, hair
color, permanents
Availability: salons

CiCi Cosmetics
4764 La Villa Marina
Unit C
Marina Del Rey, CA 90292-
7055
310-680-9696
800-869-1224
www.cicicosmetics.com
Products: cosmetics
Availability: boutiques,
discount department stores,
drugstores, mail order,
specialty stores
⊠

Cinema Secrets
4400 Riverside Dr.
Burbank, CA 91505
818-846-0579
www.cinemasecrets.com
Products: cosmetics,
theatrical makeup
Availability: beauty supply
stores, Cinema Secrets
stores, costume/novelty
stores, mail order, salons
♥ ⊠

Citius USA
4655 McFarland
Cleveland, OH 44121
800-343-9099
Products: environmentally
safe correction fluid, office
supply
Availability: independent
sales representatives, office
supply stores, Sanford
Corporation
♥

**Citré Shine (Advanced
Research Labs)**
151 Kalmus Dr., Ste. H3
Costa Mesa, CA 92626
714-556-1028
800-966-6960
Products: dandruff
shampoo, ethnic personal
care, hair care, skin care for
men and women
Availability: beauty supply
stores, drugstores, General
Nutrition Centers,
supermarkets

Clarins of Paris
110 E. 59th St.
New York, NY 10022
212-980-1800
Products: cosmetics,
fragrance for women, hypo-
allergenic skin care, nail
care, sun care, toiletries
Availability: boutiques,
department stores, specialty
stores

Clear Conscience
P.O. Box 17855
Arlington, VA 22216-1785
703-527-7566
800-595-9592
www.clearconscience.com
Products: contact lens
solutions
Availability: cooperatives,
health food stores, mail
order, supermarkets, Web
site
♥ ★ ⊛ ⊠ ⊟

Clearly Natural Products
1340 N. McDowell Blvd.
Petaluma, CA 94954
707-762-5815
www.clearlynaturalsoaps.com
Products: liquid glycerin
soap, toiletries, vegetable
glycerin soap
Availability: drugstores,
health food stores,
supermarkets, Web site
♥ ★

Clear Vue Products
P.O. Box 567
417 Canal St.
Lawrence, MA 01842
508-683-7151
Products: household supply,
window cleaner
Availability: mail order,
supermarkets in New
England
♥ ⊠

Clientele
14101 N.W. Fourth St.
Sunrise, FL 33325
954-845-9500
800-327-4660
Products: cosmetics,
fragrance for men and
women, hair care, hypo-
allergenic skin care for men
and women, sun care,
theatrical makeup, toiletries,
vitamins
Availability: boutiques,
department stores, mail
order, specialty stores
⊠

Clinique Laboratories (Estée Lauder)
767 Fifth Ave.
New York, NY 10153
212-572-3800
Products: allergy-tested skin
care, bathing supply,
cosmetics, deodorant,
ethnic personal care,
fragrance, hair care, nail
care, shaving supply, soap,
sun care, toiletries
Availability: department
stores, specialty stores

Colorations
2875 Berkeley Lake Rd.
Duluth, GA 30096
770-417-1501
Products: children's art and
school supply
Availability: school supply,
toy, and gift stores
♥

Color Me Beautiful
14000 Thunderbolt Pl., Ste. E
Chantilly, VA 20151
703-471-6400
800-533-5503
Products: cosmetics,
fragrance, skin care for men
and women, sun care
Availability: boutiques,
department stores,
drugstores, independent
sales representatives, mail
order, specialty stores
⊠

Color My Image
5025B Backlick Rd.
Annandale, VA 22003
703-354-9797
Products: bathing supply,
camouflage makeup,
cosmetics, hypo-allergenic
skin care, nail care, sun
care, theatrical makeup,
toiletries
Availability: Color My
Image stores, mail order
★ ⊠

Columbia Cosmetics Manufacturing
1661 Timothy Dr.
San Leandro, CA 94577
510-562-5900
800-824-3328
www.columbiacosmetics.com
Products: aromatherapy,
cosmetics, fragrance, hair
care, nail care, skin care,
soap, sun care
Availability: boutiques,
distributors, mail order,
specialty stores
⊠

Common Scents
128 Main St.
Port Jefferson, NY 11777
516-473-6370
Products: aromatherapy,
bathing supply, fragrance
for men and women, soap
Availability: Common
Scents stores, mail order
⊠

Compar
70 E. 55th St.
New York, NY 10022
212-980-9620
Products: fragrance for men
and women, toiletries
Availability: department
stores

The Compassionate Consumer
P.O. Box 27
Jericho, NY 11753
718-359-3083
800-733-4134
Products: cosmetics,
household supply, leather
substitutes, toiletries
Availability: mail order
⊠

Compassionate Cosmetics
P.O. Box 3534
Glendale, CA 91201
Products: cosmetics,
fragrance, toiletries
Availability: mail order
⊠

LEGEND
♥ Vegan
★ Company meets CSCA.
☙ Company uses CCIC logo.
⊠ Mail order available.
✇ Products available through
www.PETAMall.com.

Compassion Matters
2 E. Fourth St.
Jamestown, NY 14701
716-664-2207
800-422-6330
Products: aromatherapy,
baby care, companion
animal care, cosmetics,
dandruff shampoo, dental
supply, hair care, household
supply, insect repellent,
laundry detergent, razors,
skin care, sun care,
toothbrushes
Availability: Compassion
Matters store, mail order

Conair
1 Cummings Point Rd.
Stamford, CT 06904
203-351-9173
800-7-CONAIR
www.conair.com
Products: Conair hair-care
styling tools, hair care, hair
color, Jheri Redding,
permanents, toiletries
Availability: beauty supply
stores, discount department
stores, drugstores, mail
order, supermarkets

**Concept Now Cosmetics
(CNC)**
10200 Pioneer Blvd. #100
Santa Fe Springs, CA 90670
502-903-1450
800-CNC-1215
Products: cosmetics, skin
care for men and women,
sun care
Availability: distributors,
mail order

Cosmyl
1 Cosmyl Pl.
Corporate Ridge Industrial Pk.
Columbus, GA 31907
706-569-6100
800-262-4401
Products: cosmetics,
fragrance for women, nail
care, skin care for men and
women, toiletries
Availability: boutiques,
department stores, J.C.
Penney stores, Sears stores,
specialty stores

Cot 'N Wash, Inc.
502 The Times Bldg.
Ardmore, PA 19003
610-896-4373
800-355-WASH
Products: fine washables
detergent, household supply
Availability: boutiques,
cooperatives, department
stores, health food stores,
mail order, specialty stores
♥ ⊠

Country Comfort
P.O. Box 406
Fawnskin, CA 92333
909-866-3678
800-462-6617
Products: baby care,
healing salve, lip balm
Availability: health food
stores, mail order

Country Save
3410 Smith Ave.
Everett, WA 98201
206-258-1171
Products: chlorine-free
bleach, dish detergent,
household supply, laundry
detergent
Availability: available in
Canada at select
cooperatives, health food
stores, supermarkets
♥

Countryside Fragrances
1420 Fifth Ave., Ste. 2200
Seattle, WA 98101-2378
814-587-6331
800-447-8901
Products: aromatherapy oil,
essential oil, mulling spices
for cider and wine,
potpourri, simmering
potpourri, wardrobe sachets
Availability: boutiques,
department stores,
wholesale to other
companies

Crabtree & Evelyn, Ltd.
880 Winter St., Ste. 300
Waltham, MA 02451
800-624-5211
www.crabtree-evelyn.com
Products: air freshener, baby
care, fragrance for men and
women, hair care, razors,
shaving supply, toiletries,
toothbrushes
Availability: boutiques,
Crabtree & Evelyn stores,
department stores, specialty
stores

Crème de la Terre
66 County St.
Norwalk, CT 06851
203-324-4300
800-260-0700
Products: hypo-allergenic
skin care for men and
women, sun care, toiletries
Availability: boutiques,
health food stores, mail
order, specialty stores
⊠

Crown Royale, Ltd.
P.O. Box 5238
99 Broad St.
Phillipsburg, NJ 08865
908-859-6488
800-992-5400
Products: carpet cleaning
supply, companion animal
care, fragrance for men and
women, household supply,
shaving supply, toiletries
Availability: distributors,
grooming shops, mail order
♥ ✉

CYA Products, Inc.
531 U.S. Hwy. 1, Ste. 2
N. Palm Beach, FL 33408
561-882-0775
www.adzorbstar.com
Products: air freshener
Availability: boutiques,
companion animal supply
stores, distributors, health
food stores, mail order,
specialty stores
♥ ✉

Dallas Manufacturing Co.
4215 McEwen Rd.
Dallas, TX 75244
800-256-8669
www.thebrinkmanncorp.com
Products: companion
animal care
Availability: companion
animal supply stores,
discount department stores,
mail order, supermarkets,
wholesale
✉

Damp Rid, Inc.
P.O. Box 568395
Orlando, FL 32856-8395
407-851-6230
800-621-2943
www.damprid.com
Products: household supply,
mold and mildew
prevention
Availability: discount
department stores, Home
Depot, mail order,
supermarkets
✉

Decleor USA
18 E. 48th St., 21st Fl.
New York, NY 10017
212-838-1771
800-722-2219
Products: cosmetics,
dandruff shampoo,
fragrance for men and
women, hair care, hypo-
allergenic skin care for men
and women, nail care,
shaving supply, sun care,
toiletries
Availability: boutiques,
Decleor stores, department
stores, skin care salons,
spas, specialty stores

Dena Corporation
850 Nichaolas Blvd.
Elk Grove Village, IL 60007
847-593-3041
800-932-3362
Products: hair color, skin
care
Availability: drugstores,
supermarkets
★

**Deodorant Stones of
America**
9420 E. Doubletree
Unit 101
Scottsdale, AZ 85258
480-451-4981
800-279-9318
Products: deodorant stones
Availability: drugstores,
health food stores, mail
order, supermarkets
♥ ✉

Derma-E Skin & Hair Care
9751 Independence A
818-718-1420
800-521-3342
www.derma-e.com
Products: aromatherapy,
bathing supply, dandruff
shampoo, hair care, hypo-
allergenic skin care for men
and women, scar gel, soap,
sun care, toiletries
Availability: beauty supply
stores, health food stores,
mail order
✉

Dermalogica
1001 Knox St.
Torrance, CA 90502
310-352-4784
800-345-2761
www.dermalogica.com
Products: bathing supply,
herbal supplements, hypo-
allergenic skin care for men
and women, sun care,
vitamins
Availability: boutiques,
physicians, skin care salons,
spas, specialty stores

Dermatologic Cosmetic Laboratories
20 Commerce St.
East Haven, CT 06512
203-467-1570
800-552-5060
Products: bathing supply, dandruff shampoo, hair care, skin care for men and women, soap, sun care, toiletries
Availability: aestheticians, physicians

Desert Essence
9700 Topanga Canyon Blvd.
Chatsworth, CA 91311
818-734-1735
800-848-7331
Products: aromatherapy, dental hygiene, deodorant, hair care, skin care, soap, toiletries
Availability: boutiques, health food stores, specialty stores

DeSoto
900 E. Washington St.
P.O. Box 609
Joliet, IL 60434
815-727-4931
Products: private-label household supply
Availability: drugstores, supermarkets

Diamond Brands
1660 S. Hwy. 100, Ste. 122
Minneapolis, MN 55416
612-541-1500
Products: cosmetics, La Salle "10" nail treatments, nail care
Availability: discount department stores, drugstores, supermarkets

Dickinson Brands, Inc.
31 E. High St.
P.O. Box 149
East Hampton, CT 06424
860-267-2279
888-860-2279
Products: skin care
Availability: drugstores, health food stores, mail order
★ ✉

Donna Karan (Estée Lauder)
767 Fifth Ave.
New York, NY 10153
212-572-4200
Products: fragrance
Availability: department stores

Dr. A.C. Daniels, Inc.
109 Worcester Rd.
Webster, MA 01570
508-943-5563
800-547-3760
www.drdaniels.com
Products: companion animal care
Availability: companion animal supply stores, mail order
✉

Dr. Bronner's Magic Soaps
P.O. Box 28
Escondido, CA 92033-0028
760-738-7474
www.drbronner.com
Products: all-purpose cleaner, baby care, castile soaps, companion animal care, hair care, toiletries
Availability: drugstores, health food stores, mail order, supermarkets
♥ ★ ✿

Dr. Goodpet
P.O. Box 4547
Inglewood, CA 90309
310-672-3269
800-222-9932
www.goodpet.com
Products: companion animal care, vitamins
Availability: companion animal supply stores, drugstores, health food stores, mail order
★ ✉

Dr. Hauschka Skin Care
59C North St.
Hatfield, MA 01038
413-247-9907
800-247-9907
Products: bathing supply, cosmetics, deodorant, skin care for men and women, sun care, toiletries
Availability: boutiques, health food stores, specialty stores

Dr. Singha's Natural Therapeutics
2500 Side Cv.
Austin, TX 78704
512-444-2862
800-856-2862
www.drsingha.com
Products: air freshener, aromatherapy, bathing supply, car care, skin care, vitamins
Availability: boutiques, health food stores, mail order, spas, specialty stores
♥ ✉

Earth Friendly Products
44 Green Bay Rd.
Winnetka, IL 60093
847-446-4441
800-335-3267
www.ecos.com
Products: air freshener,
furniture polish, hair care,
household supply, laundry
detergent, personal care
Availability: cooperatives,
health food stores, mail
order, supermarkets
★ ✉

**Earthly Matters (First Coast
Industrial)**
2950 St. Augustine Rd.
Jacksonville, FL 32207
904-398-1458
800-398-7503
Products: air freshener,
carpet cleaning supply,
furniture polish, household
supply, laundry detergent
Availability: distributors,
health food stores, mail
order
♥ ✉

Earth Science
475 N. Sheridan St.
Corona, CA 91720
909-371-7565
800-222-6720
Products: aromatherapy,
baby care, bathing supply,
cosmetics, dandruff
shampoo, deodorant,
fragrance, hair care, hair
color, hypo-allergenic skin
care for men and women,
shaving supply, soap, sun
care, vitamins
Availability: cooperatives,
health food stores, mail
order
★ ✉

Earth Solutions
1123 Zonolite Rd., #8
Atlanta, GA 30306
404-347-9900
800-883-3376
www.earthsolutions.com
Products: baby care,
companion animal care,
natural hypo-allergenic
therapeutic skin care for
men, women, and children,
toiletries
Availability: boutiques,
cooperatives, health food
stores, independent sales
representatives, mail order,
specialty stores
♥ ✉

Eberhard Faber (Sanford)
2711 Washington Blvd.
Bellwood, IL 60104
708-547-5525
800-438-3703
www.sanfordcorp.com
Products: ink, office supply,
writing instruments
Availability: department
stores, drugstores, mail
order, office supply stores,
supermarkets
✉

E. Burnham Cosmetics
7117 N. Austin Ave.
Niles, IL 60714
847-647-2121
Products: cosmetics, hair
care, hypo-allergenic skin
care for men and women
Availability: drugstores,
health food stores, mail
order
✉

Ecco Bella Botanicals
1123 Rte. 23
Wayne, NJ 07470
973-696-7766
Products: air freshener,
aromatherapy, bathing
supply, cosmetics, dandruff
shampoo, fragrance, hair
care, household supply,
hypo-allergenic skin care,
shaving supply, soap
Availability: boutiques,
drugstores, health food
stores, mail order, specialty
stores
✉

Eco-DenT International
P.O. Box 5285
Redwood City, CA 94063-
0285
650-364-6343
888-ECO-DENT
www.eco-dent.com
Products: dental hygiene,
toothbrushes
Availability: cooperatives,
dentists, drugstores, health
food stores, mail order,
supermarkets
★ ✺ ✉

Eco Design Company
1365 Rufina Cir.
Santa Fe, NM 87501
505-438-3448
800-621-2591
Products: bathing supply,
companion animal care,
dental hygiene, furniture
polish, hypo-allergenic skin
care, laundry detergent,
paint, shaving supply, soap,
toothbrushes, wood
finishing supply
Availability:
environmentally friendly
stores, mail order
✉

Ecover
1166 Broadway, Ste. L
Placerville, CA 95667
530-295-8400
800-449-4925
www.ecover.com
Products: all-purpose
cleaner, dish detergent, fine
washables detergent,
household supply, laundry
detergent, nonchlorine
bleach
Availability: cooperatives,
health food stores, mail
order, supermarkets
✉

**Edward & Sons Trading
Company**
P.O. Box 1326
Carpinteria, CA 93014
805-684-8500
Products: hair care,
household supply
Availability: boutiques,
cooperatives, health food
stores, mail order, specialty
stores
✉

Elizabeth Grady Face First
55 North St.
Medford, MA 02155
800-FACIALS
www.elizabethgrady.com
Products: cosmetics, hypo-
allergenic skin care for men
and women, nail care, sun
care, toiletries
Availability: boutiques,
distributors, Elizabeth Grady
Face First stores, mail order,
specialty stores
✉

**Elizabeth Van Buren
Aromatherapy**
P.O. Box 7542
303 Potrero St., #33
Santa Cruz, CA 95061
800-710-7759
www.evb-aromatherapy.com
Products: aromatherapy,
essential oils, hypo-
allergenic skin care for
women, massage oil,
therapeutic blends
Availability: department
stores, drugstores, health
food stores, mail order,
massage therapists,
metaphysical bookstores
♥ ★ ✉

English Ideas, Ltd.
15251 Alton Pkwy.
Irvine, CA 92618
800-547-5278
www.liplast.com
Products: Advanced Lip
Technologies,
nonprescription therapy,
personal care
Availability: beauty supply
stores, department stores,
salons
★

Espial International
7045 S. Fulton St., #200
Englewood, CO 80112-
3700
303-799-0707
www.nomoreboss.com/products
Products: hair care,
household supply, skin care
for men and women,
toiletries
Availability: distributors,
mail order
♥ ★ ✉

Essential Aromatics
205 N. Signal St.
Ojai, CA 93023
805-640-1300
800-211-1313
www.essentialaromatics.com
Products: aromatherapy,
baby care, companion
animal care, essential oils,
fragrance, hair care, skin
care
Availability: mail order,
select stores
♥ ✉

The Essential Oil Company
1719 S.E. Umatilla St.
Portland, OR 97202
503-872-8772
800-729-5912
www.essentialoil.com
Products: aromatherapy,
baby care, bathing supply,
essential oil, fragrance for
men and women, insect
repellent, soap, soap-
making supply
Availability: cooperatives,
health food stores,
herbalists, mail order
✉

**Essential Products of
America**
8702 N. Mobley Rd.
Odessa, FL 33556
813-920-2011
800-822-9698
Products: air freshener,
aromatherapy, bathing
supply, essential oil,
feminine hygiene,
fragrance, hypo-allergenic
skin care, soap, sun care,
toiletries, vegetable oil
Availability: boutiques,
health care centers, health
food stores, mail order,
salons, spas, specialty stores
♥ ★ ✉

Estée Lauder
767 Fifth Ave.
New York, NY 10153
212-572-4200
www.esteelauder.com
Products: bathing supply,
Clinique, cosmetics,
deodorant, fragrance, nail
care, Origins, shaving
supply, skin care, soap, sun
care, toiletries
Availability: department
stores, specialty stores

Eucerin (Beiersdorf)
BDF Plz.
360 Martin Luther King Dr.
Norwalk, CT 06856-5529
203-853-8008
Products: skin care
Availability: drugstores,
supermarkets

European Gold
33 S.E. 11th St.
Grand Rapids, MN 55744
218-326-0266
800-946-5395
Products: hypo-allergenic
skin care for men and
women, sun care
Availability: health clubs
(where tanning beds are
used), salons, tanning
salons

EuroZen
10 S. Franklin Tpk., #201
Ramsey, NJ 07446
201-447-0961
Products: aromatherapy,
scented massage oil, skin
care
Availability: independent
sales representatives, mail
order
♥ ✉

Eva Jon Cosmetics
1016 E. California
Gainesville, TX 76240
817-668-7707
Products: cosmetics,
toiletries
Availability: health food
stores, mail order, spas,
specialty shops
✉

Evans International
14 E. 15th St.
Richmond, VA 23224-0189
804-232-8946
800-368-3061
www.tackyfinger.com
Products: fingertip
moistener, household
supply, janitorial cleaning
supply, office supply, skin
care
Availability: mail order,
office supply catalogs,
office supply stores
✉

Every Body, Ltd.
1738 Pearl St.
Boulder, CO 80302
303-444-2781
800-748-5675
Products: aromatherapy,
baby care, bathing supply,
cosmetics, dandruff
shampoo, dental hygiene,
deodorant, hair care, hair
color, massage oil, nail
care, shaving supply, soap,
sun care, toiletries
Availability: boutiques,
cooperatives, Every Body
Ltd. stores, health food
stores, mail order, sporting
goods stores, supermarkets
✉

The Face Food Shoppe
21298 Pleasant Hill Rd.
Boonville, MO 65233
816-882-6858
800-882-6858
Products: acne care,
aromatherapy, bathing
supply, hypo-allergenic skin
care for men and women,
soap, toiletries
Availability: cooperatives,
health food stores,
independent sales
representatives, mail order,
The Face Food Shoppe store
♺ ✉

Faces By Gustavo
1200 N. Veitch St., Ste. 812
Arlington, VA 22201
703-908-9620
800-58-FACE1
www.facesbygustavo.com
Products: aromatherapy,
baby care, cosmetics, hypo-
allergenic skin care, soap,
sun care, toiletries
Availability: boutiques,
Faces by Gustavo stores,
mail order, salons, specialty
stores
✉

**Facets/Crystalline
Cosmetics**
8436 N. 80th Pl.
Scottsdale, AZ 85258
480-991-1704
Products: skin care for men
and women
Availability: mail order
✉

Faith Products, Ltd.
Unit 5, Kay St.
Bury, Lancashire BL9 6BU
England
161-7642555
www.faithproducts.com
Products: aromatherapy,
baby care, bathing supply,
fine washables detergent,
hair care, skin care for men
and women, soap, toiletries
Availability: health food
stores, mail order
☒

Farmavita USA (Chuckles)
P.O. Box 5126
Manchester, NH 03109
603-669-4228
800-221-3496
www.sukesha.com
Products: hair color
Availability: salons

Faultless Starch/Bon Ami
510 Walnut St.
Kansas City, MO 64106-1209
816-842-1230
Products: household supply
Availability: drugstores,
supermarkets

Fernand Aubry
22, Rue de Canmartin
75009 Paris
France
01-49-260080
Products: cosmetics,
fragrance for men and
women, nail care, skin care
for men and women,
toiletries
Availability: boutiques,
department stores, salons,
spas, specialty stores

Fleabusters/Rx for Fleas
6555 N.W. Ninth Ave.
Ste. 412
Ft. Lauderdale, FL 33309
954-351-9244
800-666-3532
www.fleabuster.com
Products: insect repellent
Availability: cooperatives,
independent sales
representatives, mail order,
veterinarians
★ ☒

**Flower Essences of Fox
Mountain**
P.O. Box 381
Worthington, MA 01098
413-238-4291
Products: holistic health
care, nonprescription
therapy, vibrational
medicine
Availability: bookstores,
health food stores, mail
order, supermarkets
♥ ☒

**Focus 21 International
(Salon Visions)**
2755 Dos Aarons Way
Vista, CA 92083
800-832-2887
Products: hair care
Availability: salons

Food Lion
P.O. Box 1330
Salisbury, NC 28145-1330
704-633-8250
www.foodlion.com
Products: baby care, hair
care, household supply, nail
care, office supplies, razors,
skin care, toiletries,
vitamins
Availability: Food Lion
stores

Forest Essentials
601 Del Norte Blvd., Ste. F
Channel Islands, CA 93030
805-278-8975
800-301-7767
www.forestessentials.com
Products: body and skin
care gifts, fragrance for
women, hair and skin care
for men and women, sun
care, toiletries
Availability: beauty supply
stores, department stores,
environmentally friendly
stores, gift shops, mail order
☒

**Forever Living Products
International**
7501 E. McCormick Pkwy.
Scottsdale, AZ 85258
602-998-8888
Products: aromatherapy,
bathing supply, companion
animal care, cosmetics,
dental hygiene, deodorant,
hair care, household supply,
laundry detergent,
nutritional drinks, shaving
supply, skin care, soap
Availability: independent
sales representatives, mail
order
☒

Forever New International
4701 N. Fourth Ave.
Sioux Falls, SD 57104-0403
605-331-2910
800-977-0004
www.forevernew.com
Products: advanced care
formulations for fine
washables
Availability: boutiques,
department stores,
drugstores, mail order,
specialty stores
♥ ★ ☒

Fragrance Impressions, Ltd.
116 Knowlton St.
Bridgeport, CT 06608
203-367-6995
800-541-3204
Products: fragrance for men and women
Availability: drugstores, supermarkets

Framesi USA
400 Chess St.
Coraopolis, PA 15108
412-269-2950
800-321-9648
Products: hair care, hair color, permanents
Availability: salons

Frank T. Ross (Nature Clean)
6550 Lawrence Ave. E.
Scarborough, ON M1C 4A7
Canada
416-282-1107
Products: bleach, car care, carpet cleaning supply, glue, hair care, household supply, laundry detergent, soap
Availability: cooperatives, department stores, drugstores, health food stores, mail order, supermarkets
♥ ⊠

Freeda Vitamins
36 E. 41st St.
New York, NY 10017
212-685-4980
800-777-3737
Products: vitamins and nutrients
Availability: cooperatives, drugstores, health food stores, mail order, supermarkets
⊠

Free Spirit Enterprises
P.O. Box 2638
Guerneville, CA 95446
707-869-1942
Products: massage lotion, skin care for men and women
Availability: boutiques, cooperatives, health food stores, mail order, specialty stores
♥ ⊠

French Transit
398 Beach Rd.
Burlingame, CA 94010
650-548-9000
800-829-7625
www.thecrystal.com
Products: bathing supply, deodorant, hypo-allergenic skin care, toiletries
Availability: boutiques, department stores, drugstores, health food stores, mail order, specialty stores
♥ ★ ⊠

Frontier Natural Products Co-op
3021 78th St., Box 299
Norway, IA 52318
319-227-7996
800-669-3275
Products: aromatherapy, bathing supply, fragrance, herbal supplements, household supply, soap, toiletries, vitamins
Availability: cooperatives, health food stores, mail order
♥ ⊠

Fruit of the Earth
P.O. Box 152044
Irving, TX 75015-2044
972-790-0808
800-527-7731
Products: hair care, skin care, sun care
Availability: discount department stores, drugstores, supermarkets

Gabriel Cosmetics, Inc.
P.O. Box 50130
Bellevue, WA 98015
425-688-8663
800-497-6419
Products: baby care, contact lens solutions, cosmetics, hair care, skin care, sun care, toiletries
Availability: health food stores, mail order
★

Garden Botanika
8624 154th Ave. N.E.
Redmond, WA 98052
425-881-9603
800-968-7842
www.gardenbotanika.com
Products: bathing supply, cosmetics, deodorant, fragrance, hair care, herbal supplements, nail care, shaving supply, skin care for men and women, soap, sun care, toiletries, vitamins
Availability: Garden Botanika stores, mail order, Web site
⊠

The Garmon Corporation
27461-B Diez Rd.
Temecula, CA 92590
909-695-3848
www.naturvet.com
Products: companion
animal care
Availability: companion
animal supply stores, mail
order
✉

Garnier (L'Oréal)
575 Fifth Ave.
New York, NY 10017
212-818-1500
Products: hair color
Availability: drugstores
Note: Garnier does not test
its products on animals. It
may, however, test its
ingredients on animals.

Georgette Klinger
501 Madison Ave.
New York, NY 10022
201-641-8582
800-KLINGER
Products: bathing supply,
cosmetics, fragrance for
men and women, hair care,
nail care, shaving supply,
skin care, soap, sun care,
toiletries
Availability: Georgette
Klinger salons, mail order,
specialty stores
✉

Gigi Laboratories
2220 Gaspar Ave.
Los Angeles, CA 90040
213-728-2999
Products: skin care for
women
Availability: beauty supply
stores, boutiques, specialty
stores

Giovanni Cosmetics
5415 Tweedy Blvd.
Southgate, CA 90280
213-563-0355
800-563-5468
Products: hair care
Availability: boutiques,
cooperatives, drugstores,
health food stores, mail
order, specialty stores,
supermarkets
♥ ✉

Golden Pride/Rawleigh
1501 Northpoint Pkwy.
Ste. 100
West Palm Beach, FL 33407
407-640-5700
Products: cosmetics,
furniture polish, hair care,
household supply, laundry
detergent, shaving supply,
skin care, soap, sun care,
vitamins
Availability: independent
sales representatives, mail
order
✉

Goldwell Cosmetics (USA)
981 Corporate Blvd.
Linthicum Heights, MD
21090
800-288-9118
www.goldwellusa.com
Products: hair care, hair
color
Availability: salons

Green Ban
P.O. Box 146
Norway, IA 52318
319-446-7495
Products: companion
animal care, insect-bite
treatment, insect repellent
Availability: cooperatives,
health food stores, mail
order, specialty stores,
sporting goods stores
♥ ✉

Gryphon Development
666 Fifth Ave.
New York, NY 10103
212-582-1220
Products: fragrance,
personal care, toiletries
Availability: Abercrombie &
Fitch, Bath & Body Works,
Henri Bendel, Victoria's
Secret

Halo, Purely for Pets
3438 E. Lake Rd., #14
Palm Harbor, FL 34685
813-854-2214
800-426-4256
www.halopets.com
Products: companion
animal care, insect repellent
Availability: companion
animal supply stores, health
food stores, mail order
★

Hard Candy
110 N. Doheny Dr.
Beverly Hills, CA 90211
310-275-8099
www.hardcandy.com
Products: cosmetics, nail
care
Availability: boutiques,
department stores

Hawaiian Resources Co.
68-309 Crozier Dr.
Waialua, HI 96791
808-636-2300
www.pete.com/monoioil
Products: aromatherapy,
fragrances, hypo-allergenic
skin care for men and
women, soap, sun care,
toiletries
Availability: boutiques,
drugstores, health food
stores, mail order, specialty
stores, supermarkets, Web
site
♥ ★

The Health Catalog
1727 Cosmic Way
Glendale, CA 91201
818-790-1776
800-523-8899
www.healthcatalog.com
Products: herbal
supplements, vitamins
Availability: health food
stores, mail order
✉

**HealthRite/Montana
Naturals**
19994 Hwy. 93 N.
Arlee, MT 59821
406-726-3214
www.mtnaturals.com
Products: herbal
supplements, specialty
supplements
Availability: boutiques,
cooperatives, drugstores,
health food stores, mail
order, Montana Naturals
stores, specialty stores,
supermarkets, Web site
★ ✉

Healthy Solutions
4628-207 A St.
Langley, BC U3A 5N3
Canada
604-530-4471
Products: skin care,
vitamins
Availability: health food
stores, mail order
★ ✉

Healthy Times
13200 Kirkham Way
Ste. 104
Poway, CA 92064
858-513-1550
www.healthytimes.com
Products: baby care,
organic and vegan baby
food
Availability: baby stores,
cooperatives, health food
stores, mail order
♥ ✉

**Helen Lee Skin Care and
Cosmetics**
205 E. 60th St.
New York, NY 10022
212-888-1233
800-288-1077
www.helenlee.com
Products: bathing supply,
cosmetics, fragrance for
women, hair care, herbal
supplements, hypo-
allergenic skin care for men
and women, nail care,
shaving supply, soap, sun
care, toiletries, vitamins
Availability: Helen Lee day
spas, mail order
✉

Hemp Erotica
970 Grossmont
El Cajon, CA 92020
619-440-4361
Products: body oils,
lubricants
Availability: health food
stores, hemp stores
♥ ★ ✉

Henri Bendel
712 Fifth Ave.
New York, NY 10019
212-247-1100
Products: fragrance for
women
Availability: Henri Bendel
stores, mail order
✉

**Herbal Products &
Development**
P.O. Box 1084
Aptos, CA 95001
831-688-8706
Products: herbal
supplements, skin care,
vitamins
Availability: health food
stores, mail order
★ ✉

The Herb Garden
P.O. Box 773
Pilot Mountain, NC 27041
Products: aromatherapy,
companion animal care,
fragrance, herbal
supplements, insect
repellent, skin care, soap,
vitamins
Availability: farmers'
markets, mail order
♥ ★ ✉

h.e.r.c. Consumer Products
2538 N. Sandy Creek Dr.
Westlake Village, CA 91361
818-991-9985
Products: household supply
Availability: health food
stores, home centers and
hardware stores, mail order
♥ ✉

The Hewitt Soap Company
333 Linden Ave.
Dayton, OH 45403
513-253-1151
800-543-2245
Products: companion
animal care, fragrance for
men and women, toiletries
Availability: boutiques,
department stores, discount
department stores,
distributors, drugstores,
health food stores, mail
order, specialty stores
✉

Hobé Laboratories
4032 E. Broadway
Phoenix, AZ 85040
602-257-1950
800-528-4482
Products: hair care, hair loss
and scalp problem
shampoo, instant hand/hard
surface sanitizers, psoriasis
treatment, skin care for men
and women, supplements,
topical analgesic, weight
loss tea
Availability: boutiques,
cooperatives, department
stores, drugstores, health
food stores, mail order,
specialty stores,
supermarkets
⊠

Homebody (Perfumoils)
P.O. Box 2266
Brattleboro, VT 05303
802-254-6280
Products: fragrance for men
and women, hair care,
hypo-allergenic skin care
for men and women,
shaving supply, soap,
toiletries
Availability: Homebody
stores

**Home Service Products
Company**
P.O. Box 129
Lambertville, NJ 08530
609-397-8674
Products: fine washables
detergent, laundry detergent
Availability: mail order
♥ ★ ⊠

House of Cheriss
13475 Holiday Dr.
Saratoga, CA 95070
408-867-6795
Products: ayurvedic skin
care for men and women,
body lotion, cleansing
cream, hair oil, masks,
massage cream, moisturizer,
toner, travel packs, washing
grains
Availability: health food and
specialty stores in San
Francisco Bay area, mail
order
⊠

H2O Plus
845 W. Madison
Chicago, IL 60607
312-850-9283
800-242-BATH
www.h2oplus.com
Products: baby and child
care, cosmetics, fragrance
for men and women, hair
care, nail care, shaving
supply, skin care for men
and women, sun care,
toiletries, toothbrushes, toys
Availability: boutiques,
department stores, duty-free
shops, H2O Plus stores,
mail order, specialty stores
⊠

Huish Detergents
3540 W. 1987 S.
P.O. Box 25057
Salt Lake City, UT 84125
801-975-3100
800-776-6702
www.huish.com
Products: dish detergent,
disinfectant, floor finish,
household supply, window
cleaner
Availability: department
stores, discount department
stores, drugstores,
supermarkets

**Ida Grae (Nature's Colors
Cosmetics)**
424 La Verne Ave.
Mill Valley, CA 94941
415-388-6101
Products: cosmetics, hypo-
allergenic skin care for men
and women, Nature's
Colors: Dyes From Plants
Availability: boutiques,
cooperatives, health food
stores, i natural stores, mail
order, specialty stores
⊠

Il-Makiage
107 E. 60th St.
New York, NY 10022
800-722-1011
Products: cosmetics, hair
care, hair color, hypo-
allergenic skin care for
women, nail care
Availability: boutiques,
cooperatives, health spas,
Il-Makiage stores, mail
order, salons, specialty
stores
⊠

ILONA
3201 E. Second Ave.
Denver, CO 80206-5203
303-322-3000
888-38-ILONA
www.ilona.com
Products: cosmetics,
fragrance for men and
women, nail care, skin care
for men and women, soap,
sun care
Availability: boutiques,
department stores, Ilona
stores, mail order, specialty
stores, Web site
⊠

**i natural cosmetics
(Cosmetic Source)**
32-02 Queen's Blvd.
Long Island City, NY 11101
718-729-2929
800-962-5387
Products: cosmetics, hair
care, hypo-allergenic skin
care for men and women,
shaving supply, sun care,
toiletries
Availability: General
Nutrition Centers, i natural
stores

Innovative Formulations
1810 S. Sixth Ave.
S. Tucson, AZ 85713
520-628-1553
Products: architectural
paint, household supply,
nail polish remover, paint,
roof coatings, roofing
material
Availability: mail order
♥ ✉

International Rotex
7171 Telegraph Rd.
Los Angeles, CA 90040-
3227
Products: correction fluid,
office supply
Availability: cooperatives,
discount department stores,
drugstores, supermarkets,
wholesale distributors
♥

**International Vitamin
Corporation**
209 40th St.
Irvington, NJ 07111
201-371-7300
Products: vitamins
Availability: health food
stores, mail order
✉

InterNatural
P.O. Box 1008
Silver Lake, WI 53170
414-889-8501
800-548-3824
www.internatural.com
Products: aromatherapy,
condoms, cosmetics,
dandruff shampoo, dental
hygiene, feminine hygiene,
furniture polish, hair color,
insect repellent, laundry
detergent, nail care, skin
care, sun care, toiletries
Availability: mail order,
Web site
✉

IQ Products Company
16212 State Hwy. 249
Houston, TX 77086
281-444-6454
Products: car care, cleaning
supply, hair care, insect
repellent
Availability: discount
department stores,
drugstores, supermarkets

Island Dog Cosmetics
3 Milltown Ct.
Union, NJ 07083
908-851-0330
Products: cosmetics
Availability: specialty stores
★

IV Trail Products
P.O. Box 1033
Sykesville, MD 21784
410-795-8989
Products: companion
animal care for horses
Availability: mail order
♥ ✉

Jacki's Magic Lotion
258 A St., #7A
Ashland, OR 97520
541-488-1388
Products: aromatherapy,
baby care, ethnic personal
care, massage lotions,
shaving supply, skin care for
men and women, toiletries
Availability: cooperatives,
health food stores, mail
order
★ ✉

James Austin Company
P.O. Box 827
115 Downieville Rd.
Mars, PA 16046
724-625-1535
800-245-1942
Products: all-purpose
cleaner, bleach, carpet
cleaning supply, glass
cleaner, household supply,
laundry detergent, oven
cleaner
Availability: discount
department stores,
drugstores, supermarkets

Jane (Estée Lauder)
767 Fifth Ave.
New York, NY 10153
212-572-4200
www.janecosmetics.com
Products: cosmetics
Availability: department
stores, drugstores

37

Jason Natural Cosmetics
8468 Warner Dr.
Culver City, CA 90232-2484
310-838-7543
800-JASON-05
www.jason-natural.com
Products: aromatherapy, bathing supply, dandruff shampoo, deodorant, feminine hygiene, fragrance, hair care, hair color, hypo-allergenic skin care, insect repellent, soap, sun care
Availability: cooperatives, health food stores, mail order, Web site
★ ✉

J.C. Garet
2471 Coral St.
Vista, CA 92083
619-598-0505
800-548-9770
Products: household supply, laundry detergent
Availability: boutiques, cooperatives, department stores, distributors, drugstores, health food stores, mail order, supermarkets, uniform stores
✉

Jeanne Rose Aromatherapy
219 Carl St.
San Francisco, CA 94117-3804
415-564-6785
Products: aromatherapy, companion animal care, herbal supplements, hypo-allergenic skin care for men and women, oil, toiletries
Availability: boutiques, cooperatives, health food stores, independent sales representatives, mail order, specialty stores
✉

Jennifer Tara Cosmetics
775 E. Blithedale, #195
Mill Valley, CA 94941
800-818-8272
Products: cosmetics, skin care
Availability: mail order
★ ✉

Jessica McClintock
1400 16th St.
San Francisco, CA 94103-5181
415-553-8200
Products: fragrance for women
Availability: department stores, Jessica McClintock boutiques, mail order
✉

Jheri Redding (Conair)
1 Cummings Point Rd.
Stamford, CT 06904
203-351-9000
800-7-CONAIR
Products: Conair hair-care styling tools, hair care, permanents, toiletries
Availability: beauty supply stores, discount department stores, drugstores, supermarkets

Joe Blasco Cosmetics
7340 Greenbriar Pkwy.
Orlando, FL 32819
407-363-7070
800-553-1520
www.joeblasco.com
Products: cosmetics
Availability: beauty supply stores, boutiques, Joe Blasco stores, mail order, salons, spas, specialty stores
✉

John Amico Expressive Hair Care Products
4731 W. 136th St.
Crestwood, IL 60445
708-824-4000
800-676-5264
www.johnamico.com
Products: dandruff shampoo, ethnic products, hair care, hair color, herbal supplements, permanents, vitamins
Availability: mail order, salons
✉

John Paul Mitchell Systems
9701 Wilshire Blvd.
Ste. 1205
Beverly Hills, CA 90212
310-248-3888
800-321-JPMS
Products: hair care, skin care, sun care
Availability: salons
♥ ★

JOICO Laboratories
P.O. Box 42308
Los Angeles, CA 90042-0308
626-968-6111
800-44-JOICO
www.joico.com
Products: hair care, hair color, permanents
Availability: salons
♥

Jolen Creme Bleach
25 Walls Dr.
P.O. Box 458
Fairfield, CT 06430
203-259-8779
Products: Jolen Creme Bleach for facial and body hair
Availability: discount department stores, drugstores, supermarkets

J.R. Liggett, Ltd.
R.R. 2, Box 911
Cornish, NH 03745
603-675-2055
www.jrliggett.com
Products: dandruff
shampoo, hair care
Availability: boutiques,
cooperatives, drugstores,
health food stores,
independent sales
representatives, mail order,
specialty stores
♥ ★ ✉

Jurlique Cosmetics
2714 Apple Valley Rd. N.E.
Atlanta, GA 30319-3139
800-854-1110
www.jurlique.com
Products: baby care,
cosmetics, dandruff oil, hair
care, household supply, sun
care, toiletries
Availability: mail order,
salons, spas
✉

Katonah Scentral
51 Katonah Ave.
Katonah, NY 10536
914-232-7519
Products: aromatherapy,
baby care, dental hygiene,
essential oil, fragrance for
men and women, hair care,
hair color, shaving supply,
toiletries, toothbrushes
Availability: Katonah
Scentral stores, mail order
✉

K.B. Products
20 N. Railroad Ave.
San Mateo, CA 94401
415-344-6500
800-342-4321
Products: companion
animal care, dandruff
shampoo, hair care, hand
lotion
Availability: companion
animal supply stores, K.B.
stores, mail order
✉

Kenic Pet Products
400 Lincoln St.
Lawrenceburg, KY 40342-
1282
800-228-7387
Products: companion
animal care
Availability: companion
animal supply stores,
drugstores, grooming shops,
hardware stores, health
food stores, independent
sales representatives, mail
order, veterinarians
✉

**Ken Lange No-Thio
Permanent Waves & Hair**
7112 N. 15th Pl., Ste. 1
Phoenix, AZ 85020
800-486-3033
Products: hair care,
permanents
Availability: salons
♥

Kenra
6501 Julian Ave.
Indianapolis, IN 46219
317-356-6491
800-428-8073
Products: ethnic personal
care, hair care
Availability: salons

Kiehl's Since 1851
109 Third Ave.
New York, NY 10003
973-244-9828
800-KIEHLS1
Products: baby care,
cosmetics, fragrance for
men and women, hair care,
skin care, sun care
Availability: department
stores, Kiehl's stores, mail
order
✉

Kiss My Face
P.O. Box 224
144 Main St.
Gardiner, NY 12525
914-255-0884
800-262-KISS
www.kissmyface.com
Products: baby care,
cosmetics, hair care,
shaving supply, skin care for
men and women, sun care,
toiletries
Availability: boutiques,
cooperatives, drugstores,
health food stores, mail
order, massage therapists,
salons
★ ✉

Kleen Brite Laboratories
200 State St.
Brockport, NY 14420
716-637-0630
800-223-1473
www.kleenbrite.com
Products: bleach, fine
washables detergent,
household supply
Availability: cooperatives,
drugstores, supermarkets

KMS Research
P.O. Box 496040
Redding, CA 96049-6040
530-244-6000
800-DIAL-KMS
www.kmshaircare.com
Products: dandruff
shampoo, hair care,
permanents
Availability: salons
★

KSA Jojoba
19025 Parthenia St., #200
Dept. PE
Northridge, CA 91324
818-701-1534
www.jojoba-ksa.com
Products: aromatherapy,
baby care, bathing supply,
companion animal care,
cosmetics, fragrance, hair
care, skin care, soap, sun
care, toiletries
Availability: mail order
♥ ★ ✉

LaCrista
P.O. Box 240
Davidsonville, MD 21035
410-956-4447
800-888-2231
www.Lacrista.com
Products: aromatherapy,
baby care, hypo-allergenic
skin care for men and
women, soap, toiletries
Availability: health food
stores, mail order, specialty
stores, supermarkets, Web
site
♥ ✉

Lady of the Lake
P.O. Box 7140
Brookings, OR 97415
541-469-3354
Products: aromatherapy,
books, homeopathic
remedies, water treatment
systems
Availability: health food
stores, independent sales
representatives, mail order
♥ ★ ✉

Lakon Herbals
RR 1, Box 4710
Montpelier, VT 05602
802-223-5563
Products: aromatherapy,
baby care, insect repellent,
personal care
Availability: health food
stores, mail order
★

LaNatura
425 N. Bedford Dr.
Beverly Hills, CA 90210
310-271-5616
800-352-6288
Products: baby care,
bathing supply, cosmetics,
fragrance for women, skin
care, soap, toiletries
Availability: boutiques,
health food stores, hotel
private label, LaNatura
stores, mail order, specialty
stores
♥ ✉

Lancôme (L'Oréal)
575 Fifth Ave.
New York, NY 10017
212-818-1500
Products: cosmetics, sun
care
Availability: department
stores
Note: Lancôme does not
test its products on animals.
It may, however, test its
ingredients on animals.

Lander Co., Inc.
106 Grand Ave.
Englewood, NJ 07631
201-568-9700
800-4-LANDER
www.lander-hbc.com
Products: baby care,
bathing supply, dandruff
shampoo, ethnic personal
care, hair care, shaving
supply, toiletries
Availability: discount
department stores,
drugstores, supermarkets

**L'anza Research
International**
935 W. Eighth St.
Azusa, CA 91702
800-423-0307
www.lanza.com
Products: dandruff
shampoo, hair care, hair
color, permanents
Availability: salons
♥

La Prairie
31 W. 52nd St.
New York, NY 10019
212-459-1600
800-821-5718
Products: cosmetics,
fragrance for men and
women, skin care for
women, sun care
Availability: boutiques,
department stores, specialty
stores

Lee Pharmaceuticals
1434 Santa Anita Ave.
S. El Monte, CA 91733
800-950-5337
Products: Bikini Bare
depilatory, Creamalin
antacid, Lee acrylic nails,
nail care, Nose Better,
Peterson's ointment, Saxton
aftershave cream, Sundance
aloe, Zip hair remover
Availability: boutiques,
drugstores, supermarkets

**Levlad/Nature's Gate
Herbal Cosmetics**
9200 Mason Ave.
Chatsworth, CA 91311
818-882-2951
800-327-2012
www.levlad.com
Products: aromatherapy,
bathing supply, dental
hygiene, deodorant, hair
care, hypo-allergenic skin
care for women, shaving
supply, soap, sun care
Availability: discount
department stores, health
food stores, mail order,
supermarkets
★ ⊠

Liberty Natural Products
8120 S.E. Stock St.
Portland, OR 97215-2346
503-256-1227
800-289-8427
www.libertynatural.com
Products: air freshener,
aromatherapy, baby care,
bathing supply, dental
hygiene, deodorant,
fragrance, hair care,
household supply, insect
repellent, nail care, skin
care, soap, toiletries,
vitamins
Availability: boutiques,
cooperatives, discount
department stores,
drugstores, health food
stores, specialty stores,
supermarkets
♥

Life Dynamics
8512 Baxter Pl.
Burnaby, BC V5A 4T8
Canada
800-977-9664
Products: hair care, hypo-
allergenic skin care for men
and women, natural color
protection, toiletries
Availability: distributors,
mail order, specialty stores
⊠

Life Tree Products
P.O. Box 1203
Sebastopol, CA 95473
707-588-0755
Products: all-purpose
cleaning supply, bathing
supply, dish detergent,
laundry detergent, soap,
toiletries
Availability: cooperatives,
drugstores, health food
stores, mail order,
supermarkets
♥ ⊠

Lightning Products
1900 Erie St.
N. Kansas City, MO 64116
816-221-3183
Products: carpet cleaning
supply, companion animal
care, household supply
Availability: companion
animal supply stores, health
food stores, mail order
⊠

Lily of Colorado
P.O. Box 12471
Denver, CO 80212
303-455-4194
www.lilyofcolorado.com
Products: purely botanical
skin care
Availability: health food
stores, mail order
⊠

**Lime-O-Sol Company (The
Works)**
P.O. Box 395
Ashley, IN 46705
219-587-9151
Products: drain opener,
household supply
Availability: department
stores, discount department
stores, drugstores,
supermarkets
★

**Little Forest Natural Baby
Products**
1501 N. Broadway, Ste. 360
Walnut Creek, CA 94596
925-944-2970
888-329-BABY
www.littleforest.com
Products: baby care
Availability: baby
boutiques, health food
stores, independent sales
representatives, mail order
♥ ★ ⊠

Liz Claiborne Cosmetics
1441 Broadway
New York, NY 10018
212-354-4900
Products: bathing supply,
deodorant, fragrance,
shaving supply, soap,
toiletries
Availability: department
stores, Liz Claiborne stores

Lobob Laboratories
1440 Atteberry Ln.
San Jose, CA 95131-1410
408-432-0580
800-83-LOBOB
www.loboblabs.com
Products: hard and soft
contact lens cleaner,
soaking solution, wetting
solution
Availability: discount
department stores,
drugstores, mail order,
supermarkets
♥ ★ ✉

Logona USA
554-E Riverside Dr.
Asheville, NC 28801
704-252-1420
800-648-6654
Products: baby care,
dandruff shampoo, dental
hygiene, fragrance for men,
hair care, hair color, hypo-
allergenic skin care for men
and women, shaving
supply, sun care, toiletries
Availability: boutiques,
cooperatives, health food
stores, mail order, specialty
stores
✉

L'Oréal U.S.A.
575 Fifth Ave.
New York, NY 10017
212-818-1500
www.lorealcosmetics.com
Products: cosmetics,
fragrance for men and
women, hair care, hair
color, hypo-allergenic skin
care for men and women,
nail care, permanents,
toiletries
Availability: boutiques,
department stores, discount
department stores,
drugstores, specialty stores,
supermarkets
Note: L'Oréal does not test
its products on animals. It
may, however, test its
ingredients on animals.

Lotus Light
1100 Lotus Dr.
Silver Lake, WI 53170
414-889-8501
800-548-3824
www.internatural.com
Products: aromatherapy,
baby care, companion
animal care,
condoms/lubricants,
cosmetics, dental hygiene,
feminine hygiene,
fragrance, hair care, herbal
supplements, insect
repellent, skin care, soap,
toothbrushes, vitamins
Availability: cooperatives,
drugstores, health food
stores, mail order, specialty
stores, supermarkets
✉

Louise Bianco Skin Care
13655 Chandler Blvd.
Sherman Oaks, CA 91401
818-786-2700
800-782-3067
www.louisebianco.com
Products: bathing supply,
deodorant, hypo-allergenic
skin care for men and
women, sun care, toiletries
Availability: mail order,
salons, Web site
★ ✉

M.A.C. Cosmetics
100 Alden Rd.
Markhem, ON L3R 4C1
Canada
416-924-0598
800-387-6707
www.maccosmetics.com
Products: cosmetics, ethnic
personal care, hair care,
hypo-allergenic skin care
for men and women, nail
care, theatrical makeup
Availability: department
stores, M.A.C. Cosmetics
stores

Magick Botanicals
3412 W. MacArthur Blvd., #K
Santa Ana, CA 92704
714-957-0674
800-237-0674
www.magickbotanicals.com
Products: baby care, hair
care, skin care for men and
women, toiletries
Availability: health food
stores, mail order
♥ ✉

LEGEND

♥ Vegan

★ Company meets CSCA.

☜ Company uses CCIC logo.

✉ Mail order available.

🖅 Products available through
www.PETAMall.com.

From nature
without cruelty.

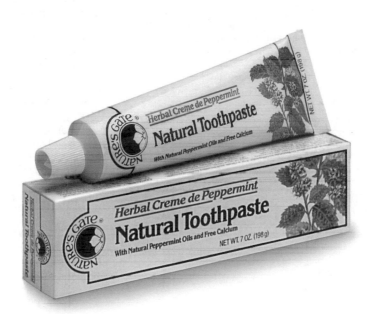

The Magic of Aloe
7300 N. Crescent Blvd.
Pennsauken, NJ 08110
856-662-3334
800-257-7770
www.magicofaloe.com
Products: bathing supply,
cosmetics, hair care,
shaving supply, skin care for
men and women, soap, sun
care, toiletries, vitamins
Availability: independent
sales representatives, mail
order, salons, Web site
⊠

Mallory Pet Supplies
118 Atrisco Dr. S.W.
Albuquerque, NM 87105
505-836-4033
800-824-4464
Products: companion
animal care
Availability: companion
animal supply stores, mail
order
⊠

**Manic Panic (Tish &
Snooky's)**
2107 Borden Ave., 4th Fl.
Long Island City, NY 11101
212-941-0656
800-95-MANIC
Products: cosmetics, hair
bleach, hair color, nail care
Availability: department
stores, drugstores, health
food stores, mail order
⊠

Marcal Paper Mills
1 Market St.
Elmwood Park, NJ 07407
201-796-4000
www.marcalpaper.com
Products: household paper,
toilet paper
Availability: drugstores,
supermarkets
♥

Marché Image Corporation
P.O. Box 1010
Bronxville, NY 10708
914-793-2093
800-753-9980
Products: hypo-allergenic
skin care for men and
women, sun care
Availability: independent
sales representatives, mail
order
⊠

Marilyn Miglin Institute
112 E. Oak St.
Chicago, IL 60611
312-943-1120
800-662-1120
Products: cosmetics,
fragrance for men and
women, skin care
Availability: mail order,
Marilyn Miglin Institute,
sales consultants
⊠

Mary Kay
16251 Dallas Pkwy.
Dallas, TX 75248-2696
972-687-6300
800-MARYKAY
www.marykay.com
Products: bathing supply,
cosmetics, fragrance, nail
care, skin care, sun care,
vitamins
Availability: independent
sales representatives
★

**Masada Marketing
Company**
P.O. Box 4118
Chatsworth, CA 91313
818-717-8300
800-368-8811
www.masada-spa.com
Products: Dead Sea mineral
bath salts
Availability: cooperatives,
health food stores, mail
order
♥ ⊠

Mastey de Paris
25413 Rye Canyon Rd.
Valencia, CA 91355
661-257-4814
800-6-MASTEY
www.mastey.com
Products: dandruff
shampoo, hair care, hair
color, permanents, skin
care, sun care, toiletries
Availability: beauty schools,
mail order, salons
⊠

Matrix Essentials (L'Oréal)
30601 Carter St.
Solon, OH 44139
800-282-2822
www.MatrixEssentials.com
Products: cosmetics,
dandruff shampoo, hair
care, hair color, hypo-
allergenic skin care for men
and women, nail care,
permanents, toiletries
Availability: salons
Note: Matrix does not test
its products on animals. It
may, however, test its
ingredients on animals.

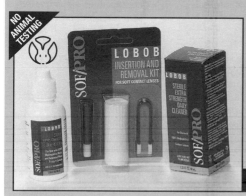
Maybelline
575 Fifth Ave.
New York, NY 10017
800-944-0730
Products: cosmetics, ethnic personal care
Availability: drugstores, supermarkets

Meadow View Garden
P.O. Box 407
Wyoming, RI 02898
800-499-7037
Products: skin care, toiletries
Availability: health food stores
♥

Mehron
100 Red Schoolhouse Rd.
Chestnut Ridge, NY 10977
914-426-1700
800-332-9955
Products: cosmetics, theatrical makeup
Availability: boutiques, costume/novelty stores, mail order, party supply stores, specialty stores
✉

Mère Cie
1100 Soscol Ferry Rd.
Ste. 3
Napa, CA 94558
707-257-8510
800-832-4544
www.merecie.com
Products: aromatherapy, fragrance for men and women
Availability: boutiques, health food stores, independent sales representatives, mail order, specialty stores, Web site
★ ✉

Merle Norman
9130 Bellanca Ave.
Los Angeles, CA 90045
310-641-3000
www.merlenorman.com
Products: cosmetics, skin care
Availability: Merle Norman salons

Mia Rose Products
177-F Riverside Ave.
Newport Beach, CA 92663
714-662-5465
800-292-6339
www.miarose.com
Products: aromatherapy, household supply
Availability: boutiques, cooperatives, distributors, drugstores, health food stores, mail order, specialty stores, supermarkets, Web site
♥ ★ ⊠

Michael's Naturopathic Programs
6203 Woodlake Ctr.
San Antonio, TX 78244
210-661-8311
800-525-9643
www.michaelshealth.com
Products: cosmetics, herbs, insect repellent, skin care, vitamins
Availability: health food stores
★

Michelle Lazár Cosmetics
755 S. Lugo Ave.
San Bernardino, CA 92048
909-888-6310
Products: skin care
Availability: health food stores, mail order
⊠

Micro Balanced Products
225 Country Rd.
Tenafly, NJ 07670
800-626-7888
Products: hypo-allergenic skin care for men and women, sun care, toiletries
Availability: health food stores, mail order
♥ ⊠

Mill Creek Botanicals
620 Airpark Rd.
Napa, CA 94558
800-447-6758
www.millcreekbotanicals.com
Products: bathing supply, dandruff shampoo, deodorant, hair care, herbal supplements, shaving supply, skin care for women, soap, sun care, toiletries, vitamins
Availability: drugstores, health food stores, supermarkets

Mira Linder Spa in the City
29935 Northwestern Hwy.
Southfield, MI 48034
800-321-8860
Products: cosmetics, hypo-allergenic skin care for men and women, nail care
Availability: mail order, Mira Linder Spa in the City stores
⊠

Montagne Jeunesse
Eco-Factory, Off Valley Way
Llansamlet, Swansea SA6 8QP
Wales, Great Britain
01792-310306
Products: aromatherapy, bathing supply, depilatory, lotions, skin care for women, soap, toiletries
Availability: boutiques, cooperatives, department stores, discount department stores, drugstores, health food stores, independent sales representatives, specialty stores, supermarkets
★

Montana Naturals/HealthRite
19994 Hwy. 93 N.
Arlee, MT 59821
406-726-3214
www.mtnaturals.com
Products: herbal supplements, specialty supplements
Availability: boutiques, cooperatives, drugstores, health food stores, mail order, Montana Naturals stores, specialty stores, supermarkets, Web site
★ ⊠

Mother's Little Miracle
27520 Hawthorne Blvd.
Ste. 125
Rolling Hills Estates, CA 90274
310-544-7125
Products: air freshener, baby care, children's stain and odor remover and prewash, spit-up remover
Availability: boutiques, discount department stores, distributors, drugstores, mail order, specialty stores
♥ ⊠

Mountain Ocean, Ltd.
5150 Valmont Rd.
Boulder, CO 80301
303-444-2781
www.mountainocean.com
Products: baby care
(prenatal), hair care,
toiletries
Availability: health food
stores, mail order,
supermarkets
✉

Mr. Christal's
10877 Wilshire Blvd
12th Fl.
Los Angeles, CA 90024
310-824-2508
800-426-0108
www.mrchristals.com
Products: companion
animal care
Availability: mail order
✉

Murad, Inc.
2121 Rosecrans Ave.
5th Fl.
El Segundo, CA 90245
310-726-3344
Products: dandruff
shampoo, hair care, hypo-
allergenic skin care, sun
care
Availability: beauty supply
stores, mail order, Murad
stores, salons, spas,
specialty stores
♥ ✉

Muse, Body Mind Spirit
2740 31st Ave. S.
Minneapolis, MN 55406
612-729-0379
877-367-MUSE
www.usemuse.com
Products: aromatherapy,
baby care, bath supply, hair
care, skin care
Availability: health food
stores, mail order, Web site
★ ✉

Nadina's Cremes
3813 Middletown Branch
Rd.
Vienna, MD 21869
410-901-1052
800-722-4292
www.nadinascremes.com
Products: aromatherapy,
bathing supply, body care,
scented body cream for
men and women
Availability: boutiques,
cooperatives, drugstores,
environmentally friendly
stores, health food stores,
independent sales
representatives, mail order,
New Age stores, specialty
stores
★ ✉

Nala Barry Labs
P.O. Box 151
Palm Desert, CA 92261
800-397-4174
Products: companion
animal care, nutritional
supplements
Availability: boutiques,
companion animal supply
stores, cooperatives, garden
shops, health food stores,
specialty stores
♥

Narwhale of High Tor, Ltd.
591 S. Mountain Rd.
New City, NY 10956
914-634-8832
800-MD-CREAM
Products: cosmetics, hypo-
allergenic skin care for men
and women, sun care
Availability: mail order,
physicians, skin care clinics
✉

Natracare
191 University Blvd.
Ste. 294
Denver, CO 80206
Products: feminine hygiene
Availability: cooperatives,
drugstores, health food
stores, mail order,
supermarkets
♥ ✉

Naturade Cosmetics
14370 Myford Rd., Ste. 100
Irvine, CA 92602
800-421-1830
www.naturade.com
Products: baby care,
companion animal care,
cosmetics, dandruff
shampoo, hair care, hypo-
allergenic skin care for men
and women, toiletries
Availability: boutiques,
cooperatives, health food
stores, mail order, specialty
stores, supermarkets
★ ◈ ✉

Natura Essentials
2845 Harriet Ave. S.
Minneapolis, MN 55406
888-606-0055
www.naturaessentials.com
Products: air freshener,
aromatherapy, essential oil,
fragrance for men and
women, hair care, massage
oil, skin care for men and
women
Availability:
aromatherapists, boutiques,
distributors, health food
stores, mail order, spas,
specialty stores
♥ ✉

47

Natural Animal Health Products
7000 U.S. 1 N.
St. Augustine, FL 32095
904-824-5884
800-274-7387
Products: air freshener, companion animal care, household supply, insect repellent
Availability: companion animal supply stores, cooperatives, health food stores, veterinarians

Natural Bodycare
23775 Monte Carlo Pl.
Poulsbo, WA 98370
805-445-9237
Products: aromatherapy, dandruff shampoo, fragrance for women, hair care, household supply, skin care, sun care, toiletries
Availability: health food stores, mail order
♥ ✉

Natural Chemistry
76 Progress Dr.
Stamford, CT 06902
203-316-4479
800-753-1233
Products: companion animal care, household supply, pool supply
Availability: cooperatives, environmentally friendly stores, health food stores, mail order
✉

Naturally Yours, Alex
1848 Murray Ave.
Clearwater, FL 33755
813-443-7479
800-546-4164
Products: companion animal care
Availability: companion animal supply stores, health food stores, holistic veterinarians, mail order
♥ ✉

Natural Products Company
7782 Newburg Rd.
Newburg, PA 17240-9601
717-423-5818
800-323-0418
Products: companion animal care
Availability: companion animal supply stores, gift stores, health food stores
♥

Natural Research People
S. Route, Box 12
Lavina, MT 59046
406-575-4343
Products: companion animal care
Availability: companion animal supply stores, cooperatives, health food stores, mail order, veterinarians
♥ ✉

Natural Science
409 W. 76th St.
Davenport, IA 52806-1322
888-EARTH-SAFE
Products: aromatherapy, baby care, cosmetics, fragrance for men and women, hypo-allergenic skin care for men and women, sun care
Availability: department stores, drugstores, health food stores, mail order
♥ ★ ✉

Natural (Surrey)
13110 Trails End Rd.
Leander, TX 78641
512-267-7172
Products: shaving supply, soap, toiletries
Availability: department stores, drugstores, health food stores, mail order, supermarkets
✉

Natural World
6929 E. Greenway Pkwy.
Ste. 100
Scottsdale, AZ 85254
602-905-1110
800-728-3388
Products: aromatherapy, car care, carpet cleaning supply, dental hygiene, furniture polish, hair care, herbal supplements, hypo-allergenic skin care, laundry detergent, sun care, toiletries, vitamins
Availability: independent sales representatives, mail order
✉

Nature Clean (Frank T. Ross & Sons, Ltd.)
6550 Lawrence Ave. E.
Scarborough, ON M1C 4A7
Canada
416-282-1107
Products: bleach, car care, carpet cleaning supply, glue, hair care, household supply, laundry detergent, soap
Availability: cooperatives, department stores, drugstores, health food stores, mail order, supermarkets
♥ ✉

**Nature de France, Ltd.
(Para Laboratories)**
100 Rose Ave.
Hempstead, NY 11550
516-538-4600
800-645-3752
www.queenhelene.com
Products: bathing supply,
hair care, skin care for
women, soap, toiletries
Availability: boutiques,
cooperatives, department
stores, discount department
stores, drugstores, health
food stores, mail order,
specialty stores,
supermarkets
♥ ✉

Nature's Acres
8984 E. Weinke Rd.
North Freedom, WI 53951
608-522-4492
800-499-HERB
Products: aromatherapy,
baby care, bathing supply,
companion animal care,
fragrance for men and
women, herbal
supplements, shaving
supply, skin care for men
and women, soap, toiletries,
vitamins
Availability: boutiques,
health food stores, mail
order, specialty stores
✉

**Nature's Best (Natural
Research People)**
S. Route, Box 12
Lavina, MT 59046
406-575-4343
Products: companion
animal care
Availability: companion
animal supply stores, health
food stores, mail order
♥ ✉

Nature's Country Pet
1765 Garnet Ave., Ste. 12
San Diego, CA 92109
619-230-1058
Products: companion
animal care
Availability: companion
animal supply stores, health
food stores, mail order
♥ ✉

Nature's Plus
548 Broadhollow Rd.
Melville, NY 11747-3708
516-293-0030
800-645-9500
Products: companion
animal care, cosmetics,
dandruff shampoo, dietary
supplements, hair care, nail
care, Nature's Plus brand,
skin care for men and
women, toiletries
Availability: health food
stores

Nature's Radiance
23704-5 El Toro Rd.
PMB #513
Lake Forest, CA 92630
949-588-9438
877-628-8736
www.naturesradiance.com
Products: deodorant, hair
care, personal care, skin
care, sun care
Availability: boutiques, mail
order, Nature's Radiance
store, specialty stores
✐ ✉

Nectarine
1011 Gilman St.
Berkeley, CA 94710
510-558-7100
800-966-3457
www.terranovabody.com
Products: bathing supply,
fragrance for men and
women, hair care, nail care,
shaving supply, skin care for
men and women, soap,
toiletries
Availability: boutiques,
specialty stores

Neocare Laboratories
33 Journey, Ste. 200
Aliso Viejo, CA 92656
714-360-1193
Products: grease trap and
septic tank control supply,
household supply, hypo-
allergenic skin care for men
and women, odor
eliminator, pool and spa
supply
Availability: cooperatives,
health food stores, mail
order
♥ ✉

Neo Soma
P.O. Box 50933
Eugene, OR 97405
541-431-3359
Products: hair care, skin
care
Availability: country clubs,
health clubs, pro shops,
sporting goods stores
♥

New Age Products
16200 N. Hwy. 101
Willits, CA 95490-9710
707-459-5969
888-7-NEWAGE
Products: biodegradable
household detergent
Availability: cooperatives,
health food stores
♥

Neway
Little Harbor
42 Doaks Ln.
Marblehead, MA 01945
617-631-9400
Products: household supply
Availability: health food
stores, mail order
♥

Neways
150 E. 400 N.
Salem, UT 84653
801-423-2800
800-998-7233
Products: cosmetics, dental
hygiene, hair care,
household supply, hypo-
allergenic skin care for men
and women, nail care,
shaving supply, sun care,
toiletries
Availability: boutiques,
distributors, mail order,
specialty stores
★ ✉

New Chapter Extracts
P.O. Box 1947
Brattleboro, VT 05302
802-257-0018
800-543-7279
www.newchapter.com
Products: ginger delivery
system, herbal extracts,
nutritional supplements,
skin care
Availability: aestheticians,
cooperatives, health food
stores, mail order,
physicians
♥ ✉

New Vision International
1920 E. Broadway
Tempe, AZ 85282
480-927-8801
Products: hair care, skin
care, vitamins, water filters
Availability: distributors
♥ ★

Nexxus Products Company
P.O. Box 1274
Santa Barbara, CA 93116
805-968-6900
www.nexxusproducts.com
Products: dandruff
shampoo, hair care, hair
color, permanents, toiletries,
vitamins
Availability: salons

Nikken
15363 Varrance Pkwy.
Irvine, CA 92618
949-789-2000
Products: skin care
Availability: specialty stores

Nirvana
P.O. Box 26275
Minneapolis, MN 55426
612-932-2919
800-432-2919
Products: aromatherapy,
hair care, skin care
Availability: cooperatives,
drugstores, health food
stores, mail order
♥ ★ ✉

Nivea (Beiersdorf)
BDF Plz.
360 Martin Luther King Dr.
Norwalk, CT 06856-5529
203-853-8008
Products: skin care
Availability: drugstores,
supermarkets

No Common Scents
Kings Yard
220 Xenia Ave.
Yellow Springs, OH 45387
937-767-4261
800-686-0012
www.yellowsprings/nocom
monscents.com
Products: air freshener, bath
crystals, companion animal
care, fragrance for men and
women, incense
Availability: mail order, No
Common Scents store
✉

Nordstrom
865 Market St.
San Francisco, CA 94103
800-7-BEAUTY
Products: Nordstrom Bath
Ltd. (bathing supply),
Nordstrom Essentials
(bathing supply), Simple
and Natural Essentials (skin
care and makeup), Single
Notes (fragrance)
Availability: mail order,
Nordstrom department
stores
✉

Norelco
1010 Washington Blvd.
P.O. Box 120015
Stamford, CT 06912-0015
203-973-0200
Products: electric razors
Availability: department
stores, drugstores,
supermarkets
♥

North Country Glycerine Soap
7888 County Rd., #6
Maple Plain, MN 55359-9552
612-479-3381
800-667-1202
www.pclink.com/nocosoap/
Products: baby care, bathing supply, companion animal care, deodorant, ethnic products, hair care, hypo-allergenic skin care, insect repellent, soap, sun care
Availability: boutiques, companion animal supply stores, cooperatives, department stores, drugstores, health food stores, mail order, specialty stores, sports supply stores
✉

N/R Laboratories, Inc.
900 E. Franklin St.
Centerville, OH 45459
800-223-9348
Products: companion animal care
Availability: distributors, mail order
✉

NuSkin Personal Care
One NuSkin Plz.
75 W. Center
Provo, UT 84601
800-487-1000
www.nuskin.com
Products: hair care, nutritional supplements, skin care for men and women, sun care, toiletries
Availability: distributors, mail order
✉

NutriBiotic
865 Parallel Dr.
Lakeport, CA 95453
707-263-0411
800-225-4345
www.nutribiotic.com
Products: dental hygiene, nutritional supplements, toiletries
Availability: health food stores

Nutri-Cell (Derma-Glo)
1038 N. Tustin, Ste. 309
Orange, CA 92667-5958
714-953-8307
Products: herbal supplements, skin care, vitamins
Availability: health food stores, mail order
♥ ✉

Nutri-Metics International
3915 61st Ave. S.E.
Calgary AB   T2C 1V5
Canada
800-267-7546
Products: cosmetics, household supply, toiletries
Availability: distributors, mail order
✉

The Ohio Hempery
7002 S.R. 329
Guysville, OH 45735
614-662-4367
800-BUY-HEMP
www.hempery.com
Products: clothing, cosmetics, hemp, skin care
Availability: health food stores, mail order
✉

Oliva, Ltd.
P.O. Box 4387
Reading, PA 19606
610-779-7854
Products: soap
Availability: health food stores, mail order
♥ ✉

OPI Products
13034 Saticoy St.
N. Hollywood, CA 91605
818-759-2400
800-341-9999
Products: nail care
Availability: beauty supply stores, salons

Orange-Mate
P.O. Box 883
Waldport, OR 97394
541-563-3290
800-626-8685
www.orangemate.com
Products: air freshener, household supply
Availability: cooperatives, department stores, discount department stores, drugstores, health food stores, independent sales representatives, mail order, specialty stores
♥ ✉

Oriflame USA
8300 W. Flagler St.
Ste. 210
Miami, FL 33144-2096
704-541-3992
Products: cosmetics, fragrance for men and women, hair care, hypo-allergenic skin care for men and women, sun care, toiletries, vitamins
Availability: distributors, mail order
✉

Origins Natural Resources (Estée Lauder)
767 Fifth Ave.
New York, NY 10153
212-572-4100
www.origins.com
Products: cosmetics, ethnic personal care, fragrance, sensory therapy, shaving supply, skin care, soap, sun care, toiletries, vegan makeup brushes
Availability: boutiques, department stores, Origins stores, specialty stores

Orjene Natural Cosmetics
5-43 48th Ave.
Long Island City, NY 11101
718-937-2666
800-886-7536
Products: cosmetics, hair care, shaving supply, skin care for men and women, sun care, toiletries
Availability: cooperatives, health food stores, mail order

✉

Orlane, Inc.
555 Madison Ave.
New York, NY 10022
212-750-1111
800-535-3628
www.orlaneusa.com
Products: cosmetics, fragrance for women, hypoallergenic skin care for women, nail care, sun care
Availability: boutiques, department stores, specialty stores

Orly International
9309 Deering Ave.
Chatsworth, CA 91311
818-998-1111
800-275-1111
www.orlyproducts.com
Products: nail care
Availability: discount department stores, drugstores

Otto Basics—Beauty 2 Go!
P.O. Box 9023
Rancho Santa Fe, CA 92067
800-598-OTTO
Products: cosmetics
Availability: department stores, direct TV marketing, mail order, QVC television

Oxyfresh Worldwide
E. 12928 Indiana Ave.
P.O. Box 3723
Spokane, WA 99220
509-924-4999
www.oxyfreshworldwide.com
Products: air freshener, bathing supply, companion animal care, dental hygiene, hair care, household supply, laundry detergent, skin care for men and women, soap, toiletries, toothbrushes, vitamins
Availability: independent sales representatives, mail order

♥ ★

Pacific Scents
P.O. Box 8205
Calabasas, CA 91302
818-999-0832
800-554-7236
Products: audiocassettes with subliminal affirmations, essential oils, toiletries
Availability: health food stores, mail order

♥ ✉

Parlux Fragrances
3725 S.W. 30th Ave.
Ft. Lauderdale, FL 33312
954-316-9008
800-727-5895
Products: bathing supply, cosmetics, deodorant, fragrance for men and women
Availability: boutiques, department stores, drugstores, specialty stores

♥

Pashtanch
567-1 S. Leonard St.
Waterbury, CT 06708
203-755-3123
Products: environmentally friendly, recycled office supply
Availability: environmentally friendly stores, office supply stores

♥

Pathmark Stores
301 Blair Rd.
Woodbridge, NJ 07095
908-499-3000
Products: air freshener, baking soda, dental hygiene, razors, toothbrushes, vitamins
Availability: Pathmark supermarkets and drugstores in Connecticut, Delaware, New Jersey, New York, and Pennsylvania

Patricia Allison Natural Beauty Products
4470 Monahan Rd.
La Mesa, CA 91941
619-444-4163
800-858-8742
Products: bathing supply, cosmetics, fragrance for women, hair care, hypo-allergenic skin care for men and women, sun care, toiletries
Availability: mail order
★ ✉

Paul Mazzotta
P.O. Box 96
Reading, PA 19607
610-376-2250
www.paulmazzotta.com
Products: cosmetics, dandruff shampoo, hair care, hair color, hypo-allergenic skin care for men and women, permanents, sun care, toiletries
Availability: mail order, Paul Mazzotta stores, salons
♥ ✉

Paul Mitchell
9701 Wilshire Blvd.
Ste. 1205
Beverly Hills, CA 90212
800-321-JPMS
www.paulmitchell.com
Products: hair care, skin care, sun care
Availability: salons
♥ ★

Perfect Balance Cosmetics
2 Ridgewood Rd.
Malvern, PA 19355-9629
610-647-7780
Products: cosmetics, fragrance for men and women, hair care, hypo-allergenic skin care for men and women, sun care, thigh-smoothing cream
Availability: distributors, health clubs, independent sales representatives, mail order, salons, spas
✉

PetGuard
165 Industrial Loop S.
Unit 5
Orange Park, FL 32073
904-264-8500
800-874-3221
www.petguard.com
Products: companion animal care
Availability: companion animal supply stores, cooperatives, environmentally friendly stores, health food stores, veterinarians

Pets 'N People (Nature's Miracle)
27520 Hawthorne Blvd.
Ste. 125
Rolling Hills Estates, CA 90274
310-544-7125
Products: carpet cleaning supply, companion animal cleaning supply, litter treatment, Nature's Miracle
Availability: companion animal supply stores, mail order
♥ ✉

Pharmagel International
P.O. Box 2288
Monterey, CA 93942
831-649-2300
800-882-4889
Products: hypo-allergenic skin care for men and women
Availability: boutiques, health food stores, mail order, salons, specialty stores
♥ ✉

Pierre Fabré
1055 W. Eighth St.
Azusa, CA 91702
818-334-3395
Products: cosmetics, hypo-allergenic skin care, sun care
Availability: drugstores

Pilot Corporation of America
60 Commerce Dr.
Trumbull, CT 06611
203-377-8800
www.pilotpen.com
Products: office supply, writing instruments
Availability: catalogs, drugstores, office supply stores, supermarkets
♥

Planet
P.O. Box 48184
Victoria, BC V8Z 7H6
Canada
800-858-8449
www.planetinc.com
Products: all-purpose cleaning supply, dish detergent, household supply, laundry detergent
Availability: cooperatives, health food stores, mail order, supermarkets
♥ ✉

PlantEssence Natural Body Care
1631 N.E. Broadway St. #235
Portland, OR 97232
503-281-4147
800-752-6898
www.plantessence.com
Products: air freshener, body oil, breath freshener, fragrance for men and women, lip balm, skin care for men and women, toiletries
Availability: boutiques, cooperatives, health food stores, mail order, specialty stores
✉

Prescription Plus Clinical Skin Care
25028 Kearny Ave.
Valencia, CA 91355
800-877-4849
Products: skin care for men and women, sun care
Availability: day spas, physicians, professional skin care salons and clinics

Prescriptives (Estée Lauder)
767 Fifth Ave.
New York, NY 10153
212-572-4400
Products: bathing supply, cosmetics, ethnic personal care, fragrance for women, skin care, soap, sun care, toiletries
Availability: department stores, specialty stores

Prestige Cosmetics
1441 W. Newport Ctr. Dr.
Deerfield Beach, FL 33442
305-480-9202
800-722-7488
Products: cosmetics, nail care
Availability: beauty supply stores, department stores, drugstores, specialty stores

Prestige Fragrances, Ltd. (Revlon)
625 Madison Ave.
New York, NY 10022
212-572-5000
Products: fragrance for women
Availability: department stores

The Principal Secret
41-550 Ecclectic St.
Ste. 200
Palm Desert, CA 92260
800-545-5595
www.choicemall.com
Products: skin care for men and women
Availability: home shopping networks, J.C. Penney, mail order
✉

Professional Pet Products
1873 N.W. 97th Ave.
Miami, FL 33172
305-592-1992
800-432-5349
Products: companion animal care
Availability: companion animal supply stores, cooperatives, drugstores, mail order
♥ ✉

Pro-Tec Pet Health
5440 Camus Rd.
Carson City, NV 89701-9306
775-884-2566
800-44-FLEAS
www.protec-pet-health.com
Products: companion animal care
Availability: companion animal supply stores, health food stores, mail order
★ ✉

Protocol ;) Cosmetics
30 Willowbrook Hts.
Poughkeepsie, NY 12603
877-NETSAVY
www.protocolcosmetics.com
Products: cosmetics, lip care, nail care
Availability: Web site
★

Pulse Products
2435 Yates Ave.
Commerce, CA 90040
310-399-3447
www.oneononebodycare.com
Products: massage oil
Availability: health food stores, mail order
♥ ✉

Pure & Basic Products
20600 Belshaw Ave.
Carson, CA 90746
310-898-1630
800-432-3787
www.pureandbasic.com
Products: air freshener, bathing supply, dandruff shampoo, deodorant, hair care, household supply, hypo-allergenic skin care for men and women, shaving supply, soap, toiletries
Availability: beauty supply stores, cooperatives, mail order, salons
♥ ✉

Pure Touch Therapeutic Body Care
P.O. Box 234
Glen Ellen, CA 95442
707-996-7817
800-442-7873
www.puretouch.net
Products: aromatherapy, fragrance for women, spa supply for massage professionals
Availability: distributors, health food stores, mail order, spas
♥ ✉

Puritan's Pride
P.O. Box 9006
Oakdale, NY 11769-9006
800-284-9123
www.puritan.com
Products: aromatherapy, companion animal care, dandruff shampoo, dental hygiene, feminine hygiene, hair care, hair color, household supply, insect repellent, nail care, skin care, toiletries, vitamins
Availability: cooperatives, health food stores, mail order
✉

Queen Helene
100 Rose Ave.
Hempstead, NY 11550
516-538-4600
800-645-3752
www.queenhelene.com
Products: bathing supply, deodorant, hair care, skin care for women, soap, toiletries
Availability: boutiques, cooperatives, department stores, discount department stores, drugstores, health food stores, mail order, specialty stores, supermarkets
★ ✉

Rachel Perry
9800 Eton Ave.
Chatsworth, CA 91311
818-886-0202
800-966-8888
www.rachelperry.net
Products: skin care, sun care
Availability: drugstores, health food stores, mail order, supermarkets
★ ✉

Rainbow Research Corporation
170 Wilbur Pl.
Bohemia, NY 11716
516-589-5563
800-722-9595
www.rainbowresearch.com
Products: baby care, bathing supply, hair care, hair color, hypo-allergenic skin care for men and women, massage oil, soap
Availability: boutiques, cooperatives, drugstores, health food stores, mail order, specialty stores, supermarkets
✉

The Rainforest Company
141 Millwell Dr.
St. Louis, MO 63043-2509
314-344-1000
800-523-FROG
www.the-rainforest-co.com
Products: aromatherapy, bathing supply, hair care, rain forest-derived gifts, soap
Availability: boutiques, health food stores, specialty stores

Ralph Lauren Fragrances (L'Oréal)
575 Fifth Ave.
New York, NY 10017
212-818-1500
Products: fragrance
Availability: department stores
Note: Ralph Lauren does not test its products on animals. It may, however, test its ingredients on animals.

Real Animal Friends
95 W. Third St.
Freeport, NY 11520
516-223-7600
Products: companion animal care
Availability: boutiques, companion animal supply stores, discount department stores, mail order, specialty stores
♥ ✉

Recycline
236 Holland St.
Somerville, MA 02144
617-776-8401
888-354-7296
www.recycline.com
Products: toothbrushes
Availability: health food stores, Web site
★

Redken Laboratories
575 Fifth Ave.
New York, NY 10017
212-818-1500
800-423-5369
Products: cosmetics, dandruff shampoo, fragrance for women, hair care, hair color, hypo-allergenic skin care for men and women, permanents, shaving supply, toiletries
Availability: salons

COMPANIES THAT DON'T TEST ON ANIMALS

Rejuvi Skin Care
360 Swift Ave., #38
S. San Francisco, CA 94080
650-588-7794
www.dalnet.se/~rejuvi
Products: hair care, skin care
Availability: dermatologists, mail order, salons, spas
★ ✉

Reviva Laboratories
705 Hopkins Rd.
Haddonfield, NJ 08033
856-428-3885
800-257-7774
Products: baby care, cosmetics, dandruff shampoo, hair care, hypo-allergenic skin care for men and women, sun care, toiletries
Availability: boutiques, cooperatives, discount department stores, distributors, drugstores, health food stores, mail order, supermarkets
✉

Revlon
625 Madison Ave.
New York, NY 10022
212-572-5000
800-473-8566
www.revlon.com
Products: Almay, cosmetics, deodorant, ethnic personal care, Flex, hair care, hair color, Jean Naté, nail care, Outrageous, toiletries, Ultima II
Availability: beauty supply stores, department stores, discount department stores, drugstores, supermarkets

Rivers Run
6120 W. Tropicana A16-357
Las Vegas, NV 89103
702-252-3477
800-560-6753
www.riversrun.qpg.com
Products: all-purpose cleaning supply, car care, carpet cleaning supply, companion animal care, graffiti remover, hypo-allergenic skin care for men and women, laundry detergent, oven cleaner
Availability: mail order, Rivers Run stores
♥ ✉

Royal Herbal
P.O. Box 391806
Mountain View, CA 94039
650-596-9933
www.royalherbal.com
Products: carpet cleaning supply, companion animal care, hair care, skin care, soap
Availability: boutiques, health food stores, mail order, specialty stores
✉

Royal Labs Natural Cosmetics
Box 22434
Charleston, SC 29413
800-760-7779
Products: aromatherapy, bathing supply, chemical-free cosmetics, hair care, hypo-allergenic skin care for men and women, shaving supply, sun care, toiletries
Availability: boutiques, health food stores, mail order, salons, skin clinics, spas, specialty stores, supermarkets
♥ ✉

Rusk
One Cummings Point Rd.
Stamford, CT 06904
203-316-4300
800-829-7875
www.rusk1.com
Products: hair care
Availability: salons

Sacred Blends
P.O. Box 634
Applegate, CA 95703
530-878-7464
888-722-7331
www.jps.net/sacred1
Products: baby care, herbal supplements, skin care for men and women
Availability: cooperatives, health food stores, mail order, Web site
★ ✉

Safeway
5918 Stoneridge Mall Rd.
Pleasanton, CA 94588-3229
510-467-3000
Products: baby care, household supply, toiletries
Availability: Safeway supermarkets

Sagami
825 N. Cass Ave., Ste. 101
Westmont, IL 60559
630-789-9999
Products: condoms (Excalibur, Peace & Sound regular, Peace & Sound ultra thin, Sagami Type E, Vis-à-Vis)
Availability: drugstores, specialty stores, supermarkets
♥

Sanford
2711 Washington Blvd.
Bellwood, IL 60104
708-547-5525
800-323-0749
www.sanfordcorp.com
Products: art supply, ink,
office supply, writing
instruments
Availability: department
stores, drugstores, mail
order, office supply stores,
supermarkets
✉

**Santa Fe Botanical
Fragrances**
P.O. Box 282
Santa Fe, NM 87504
505-473-1717
Products: aromatherapy,
botanical colognes,
fragrance for men and
women
Availability: mail order,
natural food stores
♥ ✉

**The Santa Fe Soap
Company**
369 Montezuma, #167
Santa Fe, NM 87501
505-986-6064
888-SOAPBAR
Products: hair care, soap,
toiletries
Availability: bath shops,
boutiques, cooperatives,
department stores, health
food stores, independent
sales representatives, mail
order, specialty stores,
supermarkets
♥ ✉

Sappo Hill Soapworks
654 Tolman Creek Rd.
Ashland, OR 97520
541-482-4485
www.sappohill.com
Products: soap
Availability: health food
stores
♥

**Sassaby (Jane, Estée
Lauder)**
767 Fifth Ave.
New York, NY 10153
212-572-4200
Products: cosmetics
Availability: drugstores

Schiff Products
2002 S. 5070 W.
Salt Lake City, UT 84104
801-972-0300
800-444-5200
Products: vitamin and
mineral supplements
Availability: health food
stores, mail order
✉

Scruples
8231 214th St. W.
Lakeville, MN 55044
612-469-4646
www.scrupleshaircare.com
Products: hair care, hair
color, permanents
Availability: salons

Sea Minerals
2886 Heath Ave.
Bronx, NY 10463
718-796-5509
Products: hair care,
nonprescription therapy,
personal care
Availability: health food
stores, Web site
★

Sea-renity
c/o Israel Business Centers
Tel-Aviv Hilton
Independence Pk.
Tel-Aviv, Israel 63405
972-3-520-22
Products: aromatherapy,
bath salts, Dead Sea black
mud body wraps, holistic
scrubs, shower gel, skin and
spa care for men and
women, soap
Availability: boutiques,
cooperatives, distributors,
health food stores, mail
order, specialty stores
✉

Sebastian International
P.O. Box 4111
Woodland Hills, CA 91365
818-999-5112
800-829-7322
www.sebastian-intl.com
Products: hair care, hair
color, skin care for women
Availability: salons,
Sebastian collective salon
members

Secret Gardens
39588 Little Fall Creek Rd.
Fall Creek, OR 97438
800-537-8766
Products: air freshener,
aromatherapy, bathing
supply, fragrance for men
and women, household
supply, massage oil
Availability: boutiques,
cooperatives, drugstores,
health food stores, mail
order, specialty stores
♥ ✉

Senator USA
4215 Tudor Ln.
Greensboro, NC 27410
336-856-0607
800-446-0019
www.senatorpen.com
Products: office supply
Availability: distributors
★

SerVaas Laboratories
P.O. Box 7008
1200 Waterway Blvd.
Indianapolis, IN 46207
317-636-7760
800-433-5818
www.barkeepersfriend.com
Products: household supply
Availability: discount
department stores,
drugstores, supermarkets
♥

Seventh Generation
One Mill St., Ste. A-26
Burlington, VT 05401-1530
802-658-3773
800-456-1177
www.seventhgen.com
Products: baby care, dish
detergent, feminine
hygiene, household supply,
laundry detergent,
nonchlorine bleach, 100%
recycled paper supply
Availability: cooperatives,
health food stores, mail
order, supermarkets
♥ ★ ✇ ✉

Shadow Lake
188 Shadow Lake Rd.
Ridgefield, CT 06877-1032
203-778-0881
800-343-6588
Products: air freshener,
aromatherapy, baby care,
bathing supply, car care,
carpet cleaning supply,
household supply, oven
cleaner, soap, toiletries
Availability: boutiques,
cooperatives, discount
department stores, health
food stores, mail order,
specialty stores,
supermarkets
♥ ★ ✉

Shahin Soap Company
427 Van Dyke Ave.
Haledon, NJ 07508
201-790-4296
Products: soap
Availability: mail order
♥ ✉

Shaklee Corporation
444 Market St.
San Francisco, CA 94111
415-954-3000
800-SHAKLEE
www.shaklee.com
Products: baby care,
bathing supply, cosmetics,
dental hygiene, deodorant,
hair care, herbal
supplements, hypo-
allergenic skin care, laundry
detergent, shaving supply,
soap, sun care, toiletries,
vitamins
Availability: independent
sales representatives

**ShiKai (Trans-India
Products)**
P.O. Box 2866
Santa Rosa, CA 95405
707-544-0298
800-448-0298
www.shikai.com
Products: bathing supply,
facial care, hair care, hair
color, hand and body
lotion, skin care for men
and women, toiletries
Availability: boutiques,
cooperatives, drugstores,
health food stores, mail
order, specialty stores
✉

Shirley Price Aromatherapy
P.O. Box 65
Pineville, PA 18946
215-598-3802
Products: hypo-allergenic
skin care for men and
women, pure essential oil of
therapeutic quality
Availability: health food
stores, mail order, massage
therapists, salons, spas
★ ✉

**Shivani Ayurvedic
Cosmetics (Devi)**
P.O. Box 377
Lancaster, MA 01523
978-368-0066
800-237-8221
www.shivani.com
Products: aromatherapy,
bathing supply, cosmetics,
deodorant, fragrance, hair
care, shaving supply, skin
care, soap, toiletries
Availability: boutiques,
cooperatives, health food
stores, independent sales
representatives, mail order,
specialty stores
✉

Simplers Botanical Company
P.O. Box 2534
Sebastopol, CA 95472
707-887-2012
800-6JASMIN
www.simplers.com
Products: aromatherapy, companion animal care, herbal extracts, personal care, Sierra Sage Salves, vitamins
Availability: health food stores, mail order
♥ ★ ✉

Simple Wisdom
775 S. Graham
Memphis, TN 38111
901-458-4686
Products: all-purpose cleaning supply, bathing supply, carpet cleaning supply, fragrance, hair care, household supply, laundry detergent, liquid soap, skin care, spot remover, toiletries
Availability: cooperatives, drugstores, health food stores, mail order
✉

Simply Soap
6721 Delfern St.
San Diego, CA 92120
619-287-1394
888-575-SOAP
www.simplysoap.com
Products: soap
Availability: mail order, Web site
♥ ★ ✉

Sinclair & Valentine
480 Airport Blvd.
Watsonville, CA 95076-2056
831-722-9526
800-722-1434
Products: air freshener, aromatherapy, bathing supply, foot care, fragrance for women, household supply, massage oil, shaving supply, skin care for women, soap, toiletries
Availability: discount department stores, drugstores, independent sales representatives, supermarkets

Sirena
P.O. Box 112220
Carrollton, TX 75011
214-357-1464
800-527-2368
Products: Sirena liquid and bar soaps
Availability: health food stores, mail order
♥ ✉

Skin Essentials
3625 Del Amo Blvd.
Torrance, CA 90503
310-542-4807
800-987-0908
Products: skin care
Availability: drugstores, General Nutrition Center, supermarkets, Web site

Smith & Vandiver
480 Airport Blvd.
Watsonville, CA 95076-2056
831-722-9526
800-722-1434
www.fizzmos.com
Products: air freshener, aromatherapy, baby care, bathing supply, foot care, fragrance for women, household supply, massage oil, nail care, shaving supply, skin care for men and women, soap, toiletries
Availability: boutiques, department stores, health food stores, independent sales representatives, specialty stores

The Soap Opera
319 State St.
Madison, WI 53703
608-251-4051
800-251-7627
www.thesoapopera.com
Products: aromatherapy, condoms/lubricants, cosmetics, dental hygiene, deodorant, fragrance, hair care, hair color, personal care, soap, sun care, toothbrushes
Availability: mail order, The Soap Opera store, Web site
★ ✉

Soapworks
Wicks Business Pk.
15011 Wicks Blvd.
San Leandro, CA 94577
510-357-7300
800-699-9917
www.soapworks.com
Products: baby care, hair
care, household supply,
laundry detergent, skin care,
soap, sun care, toys
Availability: drugstores,
health food stores, mail
order, Soapworks store,
supermarkets, Web site
♥ ★

**Sojourner Farms Natural
Pet Products**
1 - 19th Ave. S.
Minneapolis, MN 55454
612-343-7262
888-867-6567
www.sojos.com
Products: companion
animal care, food, and
supply
Availability: cooperatives,
health food stores, mail
order, specialty stores,
supermarkets

Solgar Vitamin Company
500 Willow Tree Rd.
Leonia, NJ 07605
201-944-2311
www.solgar.com
Products: vitamins
Availability: cooperatives,
health food stores

Sombra Cosmetics
5600-G McLeod N.E.
Albuquerque, NM 87109
505-888-0288
800-225-3963
www.sombrausa.com
Products: cosmetics, skin
care, theatrical makeup
Availability: drugstores,
health food stores, mail
order
⊠

Sonoma Soap Company
1105 Industrial Ave.
Petaluma, CA 94952
707-769-5120
www.avalonproducts.net
Products: bathing supply,
hypo-allergenic skin care,
soap, toiletries
Availability: boutiques,
health food stores, mail
order, specialty stores
★ ⊠

SoRik International
278 Talleyrand Ave.
Jacksonville, FL 32202
904-353-4200
888-574-7868
www.sorik.com
Products: hair care, sun
care, toiletries
Availability: salons
⊠

Soya System
10441 Midwest Industrial
St. Louis, MO 63132
314-428-0004
www.soya.com
Products: hair care,
permanents
Availability: beauty supply
stores, salons

**Spa Natural Beauty
Products**
P.O. Box 31473
Aurora, CO 80041
800-598-3878
Products: cosmetics,
fragrance for women, hair
care, hypo-allergenic skin
care for men and women,
sun care, toiletries
Availability: mail order, Spa
Natural Beauty Products
stores
⊠

Staedtler, Ltd.
Cowbridge Rd.
Pontyclym, Mid Glamorgan
Wales, Great Britain
0448 237421
Products: office supply,
writing instruments
Availability: office supply
stores in the U.K.

Stanley Home Products
50 Payson Ave.
Easthampton, MA 01027-
2262
413-527-4001
Products: household supply
Availability: distributors,
hardware stores

Steps in Health, Ltd.
P.O. Box 1409
Lake Grove, NY 11755
516-471-2432
800-471-8343
Products: air freshener,
companion animal care,
dental hygiene, deodorant,
hair care, household supply,
skin care for women, soap,
toiletries, vitamins
Availability: mail order
⊠

Stevens Research Salon Products
19417 63rd Ave. N.E.
Arlington, WA 98223
360-435-4513
800-262-3344
www.stevensresearch.com
Products: hair care, permanents
Availability: beauty schools, salons

Stila Cosmetics (Estée Lauder)
2801 Hyperion Ave.
Studio 102
Los Angeles, CA 90027
323-913-9443
www.stilacosmetics.com
Products: cosmetics, skin care
Availability: department stores

St. John's Herb Garden
7711 Hillmeade
Bowie, MD 20720
301-262-5302
Products: aromatherapy, bathing supply, carpet care, fragrance, hair care, hair color, skin care, soap, sun care, vitamins
Availability: drugstores, health food stores, mail order
★ ✉

Studio Magic Cosmetics
20135 Cypress Creek Dr.
Alva, FL 33920-3305
941-728-3344
800-452-7706
Products: baby care, cosmetics, herbal supplements, hypo-allergenic skin care, sun care, theatrical makeup, vitamins
Availability: boutiques, independent sales representatives, mail order, physicians, spas, specialty stores
✉

Sukesha
P.O. Box 5126
Manchester, NH 03109
603-669-4228
800-221-3496
Products: hair care, hair color, permanents
Availability: salons

Sumeru
1100 Lotus Dr.
Silver Lake, WI 53170
800-478-6378
www.internatural.com
Products: aromatherapy, baby care, personal care
Availability: health food stores, mail order
♥ ✉

SunFeather Natural Soap Company
1551 Hwy. 72
Potsdam, NY 13676
315-265-3648
800-771-7627
www.sunsoap.com
Products: aromatherapy, baby care, companion animal care, insect repellent, modeling soap for children, personal care, shampoo bars, soapmaking supply
Availability: boutiques, cooperatives, department stores, drugstores, health food stores, independent sales representatives, mail order, specialty stores
♥ ★ ✉

Sunrider International
1625 Abalone Ave.
Torrance, CA 90501
310-781-3808
Products: bathing supply, cosmetics, dental hygiene, fragrance, hair care, household supply, nail care, shaving supply, skin care, soap, sun care, toiletries, vitamins
Availability: independent sales representatives

Sunrise Lane
780 Greenwich St.
Dept. PT
New York, NY 10014
212-242-7014
Products: baby care, bathing supply, bleach, carpet cleaning supply, dental hygiene, deodorant, hair care, hair color, hypo-allergenic skin care, laundry detergent, permanents, shaving supply, soap
Availability: mail order
✉

Sunshine Natural Products
Rte. 5P
Renick, WV 24966
304-497-3163
Products: companion animal care, dandruff shampoo, hair care
Availability: cooperatives, health food stores, mail order
♥ ✉

Sunshine Products Group
12737 28th N.E.
Seattle, WA 98125
800-285-6457
Products: aromatherapy, body lotion, essential oil, herbal oil, massage oil
Availability: drugstores, health food stores, mail order
♥ ✉

Supreme Beauty Products Company
820 S. Michigan
Chicago, IL 60605
312-322-0670
800-272-6602
Products: hair care
Availability: drugstores, mail order
✉

Surrey
13110 Trails End Rd.
Leander, TX 78641
512-267-7172
Products: shaving supply, toiletries
Availability: department stores, discount department stores, distributors, drugstores, health food stores, supermarkets

Tammy Taylor Nails
18007E Skypark Cir.
Irvine, CA 92714
949-222-5516
800-93-TAMMY
www.tammytaylornails.com
Products: cosmetics, hypo-allergenic skin care, nail care, skin care, sun care, toiletries
Availability: distributors, mail order, Tammy Taylor stores

✉

TaUT by Leonard Engelman
9424 Eton Ave., Unit H
Chatsworth, CA 91311
818-773-3975
800-438-8288
www.tautcosmetics.com
Products: cosmetics, hypo-allergenic skin care for men and women, sun care, theatrical makeup
Availability: beauty supply stores, boutiques, health food stores, mail order, salons, specialty stores

✉

Ted Stone Enterprises
17790 Fonticello Way
San Diego, CA 92128
858-485-1190
800-POOF-444
Products: Poof companion animal stain remover
Availability: department stores, drugstores, mail order, supermarkets

♥ ★

Tend Skin Co.
2090 S.W. 71st Terr.
Bay G-9
Davie, FL 33317
800-940-8423
www.tendskin.com
Products: nail care, razors, shaving supply, skin care
Availability: beauty supply stores, catalogs, drugstores, mail order, salons, Tend Skin store

♥ ✉

TerraNova
1011 Gilman St.
Berkeley, CA 94710
510-558-7100
800-966-3457
www.terranovabody.com
Products: bathing supply, fragrance for women, soap, toiletries
Availability: boutiques, department stores, specialty stores

Terressentials
2650 Old National Pike
Middletown, MD 21769-8817
301-371-7333
Products: bathing supply, cosmetics, deodorant, fragrance for men and women, hair care, hair color, herbal supplements, household supply, insect repellent, shaving supply, skin care, soap, vitamins
Availability: boutiques, health food stores, mail order, specialty stores, Terressentials stores

♥ ✉

Thursday Plantation
P.O. Box 5613
Santa Barbara, CA 93150-5613
800-645-9500
Products: dandruff shampoo, dental hygiene, hair care, hypo-allergenic skin care for men and women, sun care, toiletries
Availability: drugstores, health food stores, supermarkets

Tish & Snooky's (Manic Panic)
2107 Borden Ave., 4th Fl.
Long Island City, NY 11101
212-941-0656
800-95-MANIC
Products: cosmetics, hair bleach, hair color, nail care
Availability: department stores, drugstores, health food stores, mail order

✉

Tisserand Aromatherapy
1105 Industrial Ave.
Petaluma, CA 94952
707-769-5120
www.avalonproducts.net
Products: aromatherapy, bathing supply, hair care, hypo-allergenic skin care, soap, toiletries
Availability: boutiques, department stores, health food stores, mail order, salons, spas, specialty stores

★ ✉

Tommy Hilfiger (Estée Lauder)
767 Fifth Ave., #38
New York, NY 10153
212-572-4025
www.tommy.com
Products: acne care, bathing supply, cosmetics, fragrance for men and women, hair care, toiletries
Availability: department stores

Tom's of Maine
P.O. Box 710
302 Lafayette Ctr.
Kennebunk, ME 04043
207-985-2944
800-367-8667
www.toms-of-maine.com
Products: baby care, dental
hygiene, deodorant, hair
care, shaving supply, skin
care, soap, toiletries
Availability: boutiques,
cooperatives, drugstores,
health food stores, mail
order, specialty stores,
supermarkets, Tom's of
Maine store
★ ⊠

**Tony & Tina Vibrational
Remedies**
459 Broadway, 3rd Fl.
New York, NY 10013
212-226-3992
888-TONYTINA
www.tonytina.com
Products: aromatherapy,
bathing supply, cosmetics,
lip balm, nail care, skin
care
Availability: department
stores, drugstores, mail
order, specialty stores
♥ ★ ⊛ ⊠

Tova Corporation
192 N. Canon Dr.
Beverly Hills, CA 90210
310-246-0218
www.beautybytova.com
Products: fragrance, hair
care, skin care
Availability: boutiques,
department stores, QVC

Trader Joe's Company
P.O. Box 3270
538 Mission St.
South Pasadena, CA 91030
818-441-1177
Products: hair care,
household supply, toiletries
Availability: Trader Joe's
Company stores

Travel Mates America
23750 St. Clair Ave.
Cleveland, OH 44117
216-738-2222
Products: hair care,
toiletries
Availability: private label for
hotel industry only

Tressa
2711 Circleport Dr.
Erlanger, KY 41017
606-525-1300
800-879-8737
www.tressa.com
Products: bleach, hair care
Availability: salons

TRI Hair Care Products
13918 Equitable Rd.
Cerritos, CA 90703
562-494-6300
800-458-8874
www.trihaircare.com
Products: hair care
Availability: boutiques, mail
order, specialty stores
⊠

Trophy Animal Health Care
2796 Helen St.
Pensacola, FL 32504
850-476-7087
800-336-7087
Products: companion
animal care
Availability: cooperatives,
mail order
⊠

Tropix Suncare Products
1014 Laurel St., Ste. 200
Brainerd, MN 56401-3779
800-421-7314
Products: sun care
Availability: tanning salons
♥

Truly Moist
784 S. River Rd.
St. George, UT 84790
800-243-4435
Products: hypo-allergenic
skin care for men and
women
Availability: drugstores,
health food stores

**Tyra Skin Care for Men and
Women**
9424 Eaton Ave., Ste. J
Chatsworth, CA 91311
818-407-1274
Products: hypo-allergenic
skin care for men and
women, sun care
Availability: boutiques,
department stores, mail
order, specialty stores
⊠

The Ultimate Life
P.O. Box 4308
Santa Barbara, CA 93140
805-962-2221
800-843-6325
www.ultimatelife.com
Products: herbal
supplements, mealbars,
nutritional powder, vitamins
Availability: health care
practitioners, health food
stores, mail order
♥ ⊠

Ultima II (Revlon)
625 Madison Ave.
New York, NY 10022
212-572-5000
Products: cosmetics
Availability: department
stores

65

Ultra Glow Cosmetics (Nickull-Dowdall)
P.O. Box 1469, Sta. A
Vancouver, BC V6C 2P7
Canada
604-939-3329
Products: cosmetics, sun care, theatrical makeup
Availability: boutiques, department stores, drugstores, mail order, specialty stores
♥ ✉

Unicure
4300 N.E. Expressway
Donaville, GA 30340
770-248-9092
888-UNICURE
www.unicure.com
Products: hair care, personal care, skin care, sun care
Availability: department stores, drugstores, mail order, Unicure stores
★ ✉

Un-Petroleum Lip Care
1105 Industrial Ave.
Petaluma, CA 94952
707-769-5120
www.avalonproducts.net
Products: baby care, lip care, medicated rubs, natural tinted lip balms
Availability: health food stores, mail order
★ ✉

Upper Canada Soap & Candle Makers
1510 Caterpillar Rd.
Mississauga, ON L4X 2W9
Canada
905-897-1710
Products: candles, soap, toiletries
Availability: gift stores

Urban Decay
729 Farad St.
Costa Mesa, CA 92627
800-784-URBAN
www.urbandecay.com
Products: cosmetics, hair color, nail care, theatrical makeup, vegan makeup brushes
Availability: boutiques, discount department stores, mail order, specialty stores
★ ⊛ ✉

USA King's Crossing
P.O. Box 832074
Richardson, TX 75083
972-801-9473
800-SHAV-KNG
www.shaveking.com
Products: razors, shaving supply
Availability: cooperatives, drugstores, health food stores, mail order
♥ ✉

U.S. Sales Service (Crystal Orchid)
374 W. Citation
Tempe, AZ 85284
602-839-3761
800-487-2633
Products: deodorant stones, soap
Availability: cooperatives, health food stores, independent sales representatives, mail order
♥ ✉

Vermont Soapworks
616 Exchange St.
Middlebury, VT 05753
802-388-4302
www.vermontsoap.com
Products: air freshener, aromatherapy, baby care, carpet cleaning supply, fine washables detergent, fruit and vegetable wash, household supply, hypoallergenic skin care, nontoxic cleaner, soap
Availability: boutiques, cooperatives, department stores, drugstores, health food stores, mail order, specialty stores, Vermont Soapworks stores
★ ✉

Veterinarian's Best
P.O. Box 4459
Santa Barbara, CA 93103
805-963-5609
800-866-PETS
www.vetsbest.com
Products: companion animal care
Availability: companion animal supply stores, health food stores, mail order, specialty stores, supermarkets
♥ ✉

Victoria's Secret
4 Limited Pkwy.
Reynoldsburg, OH 43068
614-577-7111
www.limited.com
Products: fragrance and skin care for women, sun care, toiletries
Availability: mail order, Victoria's Secret stores
✉

Virginia's Soap
Box 45033 RPO
Regent, Winnipeg
MB R2C 5C7
Canada
204-222-5492
800-563-6127
Products: aromatherapy,
bathing supply, soap,
toiletries
Availability: boutiques, mail
order, specialty stores
⊠

Von Myering by Krystina
208 Seville Ave.
Pittsburgh, PA 15214
412-766-3186
Products: hair color, nail
care, permanents, skin care,
sun care
Availability: boutiques,
health food stores, mail
order, spas
★ ⊠

V'tae Parfum & Body Care
571 Searls Ave.
Nevada City, CA 95959
530-265-4255
800-643-3011
www.vtae.com
Products: aromatherapy,
bathing supply, fragrance
for men and women, skin
care for men and women,
soap
Availability: boutiques,
cooperatives, department
stores, health food stores,
mail order, specialty stores,
V'tae Parfum & Body Care
stores
★ ⊠

**Wachters' Organic Sea
Products**
360 Shaw Rd.
S. San Francisco, CA 94080
650-588-9567
800-682-7100
www.wachters.com
Products: aromatherapy,
baby care, companion
animal care, hair care, hair
color, herbal supplements,
household supply, laundry
detergent, vitamins
Availability: independent
sales representatives, mail
order
⊠

Warm Earth Cosmetics
1155 Stanley Ave.
Chico, CA 95928-6944
530-895-0455
Products: cosmetics
Availability: boutiques,
department stores, health
food stores, independent
sales representatives, mail
order, specialty stores
★ ⊠

Weleda
175 N. Route 9W
Congers, NY 10920
914-268-8572
800-241-1030
www.usa.weleda.com
Products: baby care,
bathing supply, dental
hygiene, deodorant,
fragrance, hair care, herbal
supplements, homeopathic
medicines, shaving supply,
skin care, soap, toiletries
Availability: boutiques,
cooperatives, drugstores,
health food stores, mail
order, specialty stores,
Weleda store
★ ⊠

The Wella Corporation
12 Mercedes Dr.
Montvale, NJ 07645
201-930-1020
800-526-4657
Products: hair care, hair
color, permanents
Availability: boutiques,
salons, specialty stores

Wellington Laboratories
1147 Stoneshead Ct., Ste. B
Westlake Village, CA 91361
805-495-4824
Products: baby care, hypo-
allergenic skin care, shaving
supply, toiletries
Availability: boutiques,
cooperatives, department
stores, discount department
stores, distributors,
drugstores, mail order,
specialty stores,
supermarkets
⊠

Whip-It Products
P.O. Box 30128
Pensacola, FL 32503
904-436-2125
800-582-0398
Products: all-purpose
cleaning supply for home
and industrial use, carpet
cleaning supply, household
supply, laundry detergent,
oven cleaner
Availability: independent
sales representatives, mail
order
♥ ⊠

Wind River Herbs
P.O. Box 3876
Jackson, WY 83001
307-733-6731
Products: herbal medicine
Availability: clinics, health
food stores, mail order, The
Herb Store
⊠

WiseWays Herbals
Singing Brook Farm
99 Harvey Rd.
Worthington, MA 01098
413-238-4268
888-540-1600
www.wiseways.com
Products: air freshener, aromatherapy, baby care, bathing supply, deodorant, feminine hygiene, furniture polish, hair care, insect repellent, skin care
Availability: boutiques, cooperatives, department stores, drugstores, health food stores, mail order, specialty stores
✉

Womankind
P.O. Box 1775
Sebastopol, CA 95473
707-522-8662
Products: cloth menstrual pads, feminine hygiene
Availability: boutiques, cooperatives, health food stores, independent sales representatives, mail order, specialty stores, supermarket
✉

Wysong Corporation
1880 N. Eastman Rd.
Midland, MI 48642-7779
517-631-0009
800-748-0188
Products: companion animal care, hair care, shaving supply, sun care, toiletries, vitamins
Availability: health food stores, mail order
✉

Zia Natural Skincare
1337 Evans Ave.
San Francisco, CA 94124
415-642-8339
800-334-7546
www.zianatural.com
Products: aromatherapy, cosmetics, skin care, sun care
Availability: boutiques, cooperatives, health food stores, mail order, specialty stores, Web site
✉

LEGEND

♥ Vegan

★ Company meets CSCA.

☜ Company uses CCIC logo.

✉ Mail order available.

🛒 Products available through www.PETAMall.com.

CATALOGS/ONLINE STORES OFFERING CRUELTY-FREE PRODUCTS

EthicalShopper.com
2130 Sawtelle Blvd.
Ste. 308
Los Angeles, CA 90025
877-433-8442
www.EthicalShopper.com
Products: air fresheners,
aromatherapy, baby care,
bleach, car care, carpet
cleaning supply,
companion animal care,
cosmetics, dandruff
shampoo, dental hygiene,
deodorant, feminine
hygiene, fragrance for men
and women, furniture
polish, hair care, household
products, hypo-allergenic
skin care, insect repellent,
laundry detergent, office
supply, shaving supply, skin
care, sun care, toiletries,
vitamins
Availability: mail order,
Web site
✉ ☕

Green Earth Office Supply
P.O. Box 719
Redwood Estates, CA 95044
800-327-8449
www.greenearthoffice
supply.com
Products: art supply, glue,
hemp, office supply
Availability: mail order
✉

GreenMarketplace.com
5808 Forbes Ave., 2nd Fl.
Pittsburgh, PA 15217
888-59-EARTH
www.GreenMarketplace.com
Products: baby care,
bleach, car care, carpet
cleaning supply,
companion animal care,
contact lens solutions,
cosmetics, dandruff
shampoo, dental hygiene,
deodorant, feminine
hygiene, fine washables
detergent, hair care,
household supply, hypo-
allergenic skin care, insect
repellent, laundry
detergent, shaving supply,
skin care, sun care,
toiletries, toothbrushes
Availability: mail order,
Web site
✉ ☕

A Happy Planet
2261 Market St., #71
San Francisco, CA 94114
888-946-4277
www.ahappyplanet.com
Products: bedding,
household products, office
supply, T-shirts,
undergarments
Availability: mail order,
Web site
✉ ☕

The Heritage Store
P.O. Box 444
Virginia Beach, VA 23458
757-428-0100
800-862-2923
www.caycecures.com
Products: aromatherapy,
dandruff shampoo, dental
hygiene, essential oil,
fragrance, hair care, health
care items, herbal
supplements, hypo-
allergenic skin care, sun
care, toiletries, vitamins
Availability: health food
stores, Heritage store, mail
order
✉

MotherNature.com
360 Massachusetts Ave.
Ste. 103
Acton, MA 01720
800-517-9020
www.MotherNature.com
Products: all-purpose
cleaning supply, baby care,
bathing supply, bleach,
companion animal care,
condoms/lubricants,
contact lens solutions,
cosmetics, dandruff
shampoo, dental hygiene,
deodorant, dish detergent,
feminine hygiene, fine
washables detergent,
fragrance for men and
women, hair care, hair
color, laundry detergent,
shaving supply, skin care,
sun care, window cleaner
Availability: mail order,
Web site
✉ ☕

LEGEND

♥ Vegan

★ Company meets CSCA.

↻ Company uses CCIC logo.

✉ Mail order available.

☕ Products available through
www.PETAMall.com.

NoHARM
138 Main St.
Nyack, NY 10960
914-358-4242
www.noharmstore.com
Products: buttons, health
and nutrition books,
stickers, T-shirts
Availability: mail order,
NoHARM store
♥ ✉

Pangea Vegan Products
7829 Woodmont Ave.
Bethesda, MD 20814
301-652-3181
www.pangeaveg.com
Products: baby care,
companion animal care,
condoms/lubricants,
cosmetics, dental and
feminine hygiene, hair
care, household supply,
laundry detergent, nail
care, razors, skin care, sun
care, toiletries,
toothbrushes
Availability: mail order,
Pangea store, Web site
♥ ✉ ⌐

PETA
501 Front St.
Norfolk, VA 23510
757-622-7382
www.peta-online.org
Products: household
supply, laundry detergent,
soap
Availability: mail order,
PETA Merchandise
Department, PETA Mall
(www.PETAMall.com)
♥ ✉

**Physicians Laboratories
(Revival Soy)**
138 Oakwood Dr.
Winston-Salem, NC 27103
336-722-2337
800-500-2055
www.revivalhealth.com
Products: herbal
supplements, soy coffee,
soy protein
Availability: mail order,
internet
⌐

Veg Essentials
7722 W. Menomonee River
Pkwy.
Wauwatosa, WI 53213
414-607-1953
877-881-6477
www.vegessentials.com
Products: air freshener,
aromatherapy, baby care,
carpet cleaning supply,
companion animal care,
cosmetics, dental hygiene,
hair care, insect repellent,
laundry detergent, skin
care, toiletries
Availability: mail order
♥ ✉ ⌐

Wow-Bow Distributors
13B Lucon Dr.
Deer Park, NY 11729
800-326-0230
Products: companion
animal care: biscuits, insect
repellent, vegan and
vegetarian food, vitamins
Availability: mail order,
Wow-Bow Distributors
store
✉

Valuable guides available from

THE VEGETARIAN RESOURCE GROUP:

 The Vegan Diet During Pregnancy, Lactation, and
Childhood $3

 Guide to Food Ingredients $4

Vegetarian and Vegan Menu Items at Fast Food and
Quick Service Restaurant Chains $4

*To order any of these items, please send a check or money order to The
Vegetarian Resource Group, P.O. Box 1463, Baltimore, MD 21203 or call (410)
366-8343 weekdays between 9 a.m. and 6 p.m. EST to charge your order with a
Visa or Mastercard. You can also fax your order to (410) 366-8804 or place
your order at our Web site: www.vrg.org.*

QUICK REFERENCE GUIDE

CONDOMS/LUBRICANTS

CONTACT LENS SOLUTIONS

COSMETICS

HAIR COLOR

HOUSEHOLD SUPPLIES

They Smell as Amazing As They Work.

New Ultra Citra-Dish and Ultra Citra-Suds

Our products not only leave your clothes, dishes, counters, floors and air clean, they also leave behind the scent of fresh-squeezed oranges! Imagine: cruelty-free, petroleum distillate-free and icky-smell-free. Only from Shadow Lake, Inc. Naturally.

SHADOW LAKE, INC.

Shadow Lake, Inc.
P.O. Box 2597
Danbury, CT 06877
(800) 343-6588
www.shadowlake.com

©2000 Shadow Lake, Inc.
Citra-Solv, Air Scense and
Shadow Lake are registered
trademarks of Shadow Lake,
Inc. Citra-Dish and Citra-Suds
are trademarks of Shadow
Lake, Inc. All rights reserved.

HYPO-ALLERGENIC SKIN CARE

INSECT REPELLENT

LAUNDRY DETERGENT

MAKEUP BRUSHES (VEGAN)

85

SUN CARE/TANNING

THEATRICAL MAKEUP

TOILETRIES/PERSONAL CARE

WHY ARE THESE COMPANIES INCLUDED ON THE "DO TEST" LIST?

The following companies manufacture products that **are** tested on animals. Those marked with a check (✓) are presently observing a moratorium on (i.e., current suspension of) animal testing. Please encourage them to announce a permanent ban. Listed in parentheses are either examples of products manufactured by that company or if applicable, its parent company. Companies on this list may manufacture individual lines of products without animal testing (e.g., Del Laboratories claims that its Naturistics and Natural Glow lines are not animal tested). They have not, however, eliminated animal testing on their entire line of cosmetics and household products.

Similarly, companies on this list may make some products, such as pharmaceuticals, that are required by law to be tested on animals. However, the reason for these companies' inclusion is not the required animal testing that they conduct, but rather the animal testing of personal care and household products that is not required by law.

WHAT CAN BE DONE ABOUT ANIMAL TESTS REQUIRED BY LAW?

Although animal testing of certain pharmaceuticals and chemicals is still mandated by law, the arguments against using animals in cosmetics testing are still valid when applied to the pharmaceutical and chemical industries. These industries are regulated by the Food and Drug Administration and the Environmental Protection Agency, respectively, and animal tests are now required by law—laws that were developed haphazardly in the 1920s. We know that non-animal test methods exist **right now** and that these tests are more accurate in predicting toxicity than are crude, cruel tests on animals. It is the responsibility of the companies that kill animals in order to bring their products to market to convince the regulatory agencies that there is a better way to determine product safety. Companies resist progress because the crude nature of animal tests allows them to market many products that might be determined too toxic if cell culture tests were used. Let companies know how you feel about this.

Alberto-Culver (Tresemmé, Sally Beauty Supply, Alberto VO5, TCB Naturals, Pro-line)
2525 Armitage Ave.
Melrose Park, IL 60160-1163
708-450-3000
www.alberto.com

Arm & Hammer (Church & Dwight)
P.O. Box 1625
Horsham, PA 19044-6625
609-683-5900
800-524-1328
www.armhammer.com

Benckiser (Coty, Lancaster, Jovan)
237 Park Ave., 19th Fl.
New York, NY 10017-3142
212-850-2300
attmail@cotyusa.com

Bic Corporation
500 Bic Dr.
Milford, CT 06460
203-783-2000
✓

Block Drug Co. (Polident, Sensodyne, Tegrin, Lava, Carpet Fresh)
257 Cornelison Ave.
Jersey City, NJ 07302
201-434-3000
800-365-6500

Boyle-Midway (Reckitt & Colman)
2 Wickman Rd.
Toronto, ON M8Z 5M5
Canada
416-255-2300

Braun (Gillette Company)
400 Unicorn Park Dr.
Woburn, MA 01801
800-272-8611
braun_usa@braun.de
✓

Bristol-Myers Squibb Co. (Clairol, Keri, Infusium 23, Sea Breeze)
345 Park Ave.
New York, NY 10154-0037
212-546-4000
800-468-7746
www.bms.com

Carter-Wallace (Arrid, Lady's Choice, Nair, Pearl Drops)
1345 Ave. of the Americas
New York, NY 10105-0021
212-339-5000

Chesebrough-Ponds (Fabergé, Vaseline)
800 Sylvan Ave.
Englewood Cliffs, NJ 07632
800-243-5804

Church & Dwight (Arm & Hammer)
P.O. Box 1625
Horsham, PA 19044-6625
609-683-5900
800-524-1328
www.armhammer.com

Clairol (Bristol-Myers Squibb)
40 W. 57th St., 23rd Fl.
New York, NY 10019
212-541-2740
800-223-5800
www.bms.com

Clorox (Pine-Sol, S.O.S., Tilex, ArmorAll)
1221 Broadway
Oakland, CA 94612
510-271-7000
800-227-1860
www.clorox.com

Colgate-Palmolive Company (Palmolive, Ajax, Fab, Speed Stick, Mennen, SoftSoap)
300 Park Ave.
New York, NY 10022
212-310-2000
800-221-4607
www.colgate.com

Coty (Benckiser)
237 Park Ave., 19th Fl.
New York, NY 10017-3142
212-850-2300
www.cotyusinc.com

Cover Girl (Procter & Gamble)
One Procter & Gamble Plz.
Cincinnati, OH 45202
513-983-1100
800-543-1745
www.covergirl.com

Del Laboratories (Flame Glow, Commerce Drug, Sally Hansen)
178 EAB Plz.
Uniondale, NY 11556
516-844-2020
800-952-5080
www.dellaboratories.com

Dial Corporation (Purex, Renuzit)
15101 N. Scottsdale Rd.
Ste. 5028
Scottsdale, AZ 85254-2199
800-528-0849
www.dialcorp.com

DowBrands (Glass Plus, Fantastik, Vivid)
P.O. Box 68511
Indianapolis, IN 46268
317-873-7000
www.dowclean.com

Drackett Products Company (S.C. Johnson & Son)
1525 Howe St.
Racine, WI 53403
414-631-2000
800-558-5252
www.scjohnsonwax.com

Elizabeth Arden (Unilever)
390 Park Ave.
New York, NY 10022
212-888-1260
800-745-9696
www.unilever.com

Erno Laszlo
3202 Queens Blvd.
Long Island City, NY 11101
718-279-4480
www.ErnoLaszlo.com

Gillette Co. (Liquid Paper, Flair, Braun, Duracell)
Prudential Tower Bldg.
Boston, MA 02199
617-421-7000
800-872-7202
www.gillette.com
✓

Givaudan-Roure
1775 Windsor Rd.
Teaneck, NJ 07666
201-833-2300

Helene Curtis Industries (Finesse, Unilever, Salon Selectives, Suave)
800 Sylvan Ave.
Englewood Cliffs, NJ 07632
800-621-2013
www.unilever.com

Henkel Corporation (Schwarzkopf & Dep)
The Triad, Ste. 200
2200 Renaissance Blvd.
Gulph Mills, PA 19406
610-270-8100
www.henkel.com

Johnson & Johnson (Neutrogena)
1 Johnson & Johnson Plz.
New Brunswick, NJ 08933
732-524-0400
www.jnj.com

Kimberly-Clark Corporation (Kleenex, Scott Paper, Huggies)
P.O. Box 619100
Dallas, TX 75261-9100
800-544-1847
www.kimberly-clark.com

Lamaur
5601 E. River Rd.
Fridley, MN 55432-6198
612-571-1234

Lever Brothers (Unilever)
800 Sylvan Ave.
Englewood Cliffs, NJ 07632
212-888-1260
800-598-1223
www.unilever.com

Max Factor (Procter & Gamble)
One Procter & Gamble Plz.
Cincinnati, OH 45202
513-983-1100
800-543-1745
www.maxfactor.com

Mead
Courthouse Plz. N.E.
Dayton, OH 45463
937-495-3312
www.mead.com

Melaleuca
3910 S. Yellowstone Hwy.
Idaho Falls, ID 83402-6003
800-742-2444
www.melaleuca.com

Mennen Company (Colgate-Palmolive)
E. Hanover Ave.
Morristown, NJ 07962
201-631-9000
www.colgate.com

Neoteric Cosmetics
4880 Havana St.
Denver, CO 80239-0019
303-373-4860

Noxell (Procter & Gamble)
11050 York Rd.
Hunt Valley, MD 21030-2098
410-785-7300
800-572-3232
www.pg.com

Olay Company/Oil of Olay (Procter & Gamble)
P.O. Box 599
Cincinnati, OH 45201
800-543-1745
www.oilofolay.com

Oral-B (Gillette Company)
600 Clipper Dr.
Belmont, CA 94002-4119
415-598-5000
www.oralb.com
✓

Pantene (Procter & Gamble)
Procter & Gamble Plz.
Cincinnati, OH 45202
800-945-7768
www.pg.com

Parfums International (White Shoulders)
1345 Ave. of the Americas
New York, NY 10105
212-261-1000

Parker Pens (Gillette Company)
P.O. Box 5100
Janesville, WI 53547-5100
608-755-7000
braun_usa@braun.de
✓

Pfizer (Bain de Soleil, Plax, Visine, Desitin, BenGay)
235 E. 42nd St.
New York, NY 10017-5755
212-573-2323
www.pfizer.com

Physique (Procter & Gamble)
One Procter & Gamble Plz.
Cincinnati, OH 45202
800-214-8957
www.physique.com

Playtex Products (Banana Boat, Woolite)
300 Nyala Farms Rd.
Westport, CT 06880
203-341-4000
www.playtex.com

Procter & Gamble Co. (Crest, Tide, Cover Girl, Max Factor, Physique, Giorgio)
One Procter & Gamble Plz.
Cincinnati, OH 45202
513-983-1100
800-543-1745
www.pg.com

Reckitt & Colman (Lysol, Mop & Glo)
1655 Valley Rd.
Wayne, NJ 07474-0945
201-633-6700
800-232-9665

Richardson-Vicks (Procter & Gamble)
One Procter & Gamble Plz.
Cincinnati, OH 45202
513-983-1100
800-543-1745
www.pg.com

Sally Hansen (Del Laboratories)
565 Broad Hollow Rd.
Farmingdale, NY 11735
516-293-7070
800-645-9888
www.sallyhansen.com

Sanofi (Oscar de la Renta, Yves Saint-Laurent)
90 Park Ave., 24th Fl.
New York, NY 10016
212-551-4757

Schering-Plough (Bain de Soleil, Coppertone)
1 Giralda Farms
Madison, NJ 07940-1000
201-822-7000
800-842-4090
www.sch-plough.com

Schick (Warner-Lambert)
201 Tabor Rd.
Morris Plains, NJ 07950
201-540-2000
800-492-1555
www.warner-lambert.com

S. C. Johnson Wax (Pledge, Drano, Windex, Glade)
1525 Howe St.
Racine, WI 53403
414-260-2000
800-558-5252
www.scjohnsonwax.com

SmithKline Beecham
100 Beecham Dr.
Pittsburgh, PA 15205
412-928-1000
800-456-6670
www.sb.com

SoftSoap Enterprises (Colgate-Palmolive)
300 Park Ave.
New York, NY 10022
800-221-4607
www.colgate.com

3M (Scotch, Post-It)
Center Bldg., 220-2E-02
St. Paul, MN 55144-1000
612-733-1110
800-364-3577
www.3m.com

Unilever (Lever Bros., Calvin Klein, Elizabeth Arden, Helene Curtis, Diversey)
800 Sylvan Ave.
Englewood Cliffs, NJ 07632
212-888-1260
800-598-1223
www.unilever.com

Vidal Sassoon (Procter & Gamble)
P.O. Box 599
Cincinnati, OH 45201
800-543-7270
www.pg.com

Warner-Lambert (Lubriderm, Listerine, Schick)
201 Tabor Rd.
Morris Plains, NJ 07950-2693
201-540-2000
800-323-5379
www.warner-lambert.com

Companies listed in this guide that are marked with a (✓) are presently observing a moratorium on animal testing.

ANIMAL INGREDIENTS & THEIR ALTERNATIVES

PETA's list of animal ingredients and their alternatives helps consumers avoid animal ingredients in food, cosmetics, and other products. Please note, however, that it is not all-inclusive. There are thousands of technical and patented names for ingredient variations. Furthermore, many ingredients known by one name can be of animal, vegetable, or synthetic origin. If you have a question regarding an ingredient in a product, call the manufacturer. Good sources of additional information are *A Consumer's Dictionary of Cosmetic Ingredients, A Consumer's Dictionary of Food Additives,* or an unabridged dictionary. All of these are available at most libraries.

Adding to the confusion about whether or not an ingredient is of animal origin is the fact that many companies have removed the word "animal" from their ingredient labels to avoid putting off consumers. For example, rather than use the term "hydrolyzed animal protein," companies may use another term such as "hydrolyzed collagen." Simple for them, but frustrating for the caring consumer.

Animal ingredients are used not because they are better than vegetable-derived or synthetic ingredients, but rather because they are generally cheaper. Today's slaughterhouses must dispose of the byproducts of the slaughter of billions of animals every year and have found an easy and profitable solution in selling them to food and cosmetics manufacturers.

Animal ingredients come from every industry that uses animals: meat, fur, wool, dairy, egg, and fishing, as well as industries such as horse racing and rodeo, which send unwanted animals to slaughter. Contact PETA for our factsheets or check out www.peta-online.org to learn more about the animals who suffer at the hands of these industries and what you can do to help.

Rendering plants process the bodies of millions of tons of dead animals every year, transforming decaying flesh and bones into profitable animal ingredients. The primary source of rendered animals is slaughterhouses, which provide the "inedible" parts of all animals killed for food. The bodies of companion animals who are euthanized in animal shelters wind up at rendering plants, too. One small plant in Quebec renders 10 tons of dogs and cats a week, a sobering reminder of the horrible dog and cat overpopulation problem with which shelters must cope.

Some animal ingredients do not wind up in the final product but are used in the manufacturing process. For example, in the production of some refined sugars, bone char is used to whiten the sugar; in some wines and beers, isinglass (from the swim bladders of fish) is used as a "clearing" agent.

Kosher symbols and markings also add to the confusion and are not reliable indicators on which vegans or vegetarians should base their purchasing decisions. This issue is complex, but the "K" or "Kosher" symbols basically mean that the food manufacturing process was overseen by a rabbi, who theoretically ensures that it meets Hebrew dietary laws. The food also may not contain both dairy products and meat, but it may contain one or the other. "P" or "Parve" means that the product contains no meat or dairy products but may contain fish or eggs. "D," as in "Kosher D," means that the product either contains dairy products or was made with dairy machinery. For example, a chocolate and peanut candy may be marked "Kosher D" even if it doesn't contain dairy products because the nondairy chocolate was manufactured on machinery that also made milk chocolate. For questions regarding other symbols, please contact the Orthodox Union (212-563-4000) or other Jewish organizations or publications.

Thousands of products on store shelves have labels that are hard to decipher. It's nearly impossible to be perfectly vegan, but it's getting easier to avoid products with animal ingredients. Our list will give you a good working knowledge of the most common animal-derived ingredients and their alternatives, allowing you to make decisions that will save animals' lives.

Adrenaline.
Hormone from adrenal glands of hogs, cattle, and sheep. In medicine. *Alternatives: synthetics.*

Alanine.
(See **Amino Acids**.)

Albumen.
In eggs, milk, muscles, blood, and many vegetable tissues and fluids. In cosmetics, albumen is usually derived from egg whites and used as a coagulating agent. May cause allergic reaction. In cakes, cookies, candies, etc. Egg whites sometimes used in "clearing" wines. Derivative: **Albumin.**

Albumin.
(See **Albumen**.)

Alcloxa.
(See **Allantoin**.)

Aldioxa.
(See **Allantoin**.)

Aliphatic Alcohol.
(See **Lanolin** and **Vitamin A**.)

Allantoin.
Uric acid from cows, most mammals. Also in many plants (especially comfrey). In cosmetics (especially creams and lotions) and used in treatment of wounds and ulcers. Derivatives: **Alcloxa, Aldioxa.** *Alternatives: extract of comfrey root, synthetics.*

Alligator Skin.
(See **Leather**.)

Alpha-Hydroxy Acids.
Any one of several acids used as an exfoliant and in anti-wrinkle products. Lactic acid may be animal-derived (see **Lactic Acid**). *Alternatives: Glycolic acid, citric acid, and salicylic acid are plant- or fruit-derived.*

Ambergris.
From whale intestines. Used as a fixative in making perfumes and as a flavoring in foods and beverages. *Alternatives: synthetic or vegetable fixatives.*

Amino Acids.
The building blocks of protein in all animals and plants. In cosmetics, vitamins, supplements, shampoos, etc. *Alternatives: synthetics, plant sources.*

Aminosuccinate Acid.
(See **Aspartic Acid**.)

Angora.
Hair from the Angora rabbit or goat. Used in clothing. *Alternatives: synthetic fibers.*

Animal Fats and Oils.
In foods, cosmetics, etc. Highly allergenic. *Alternatives: olive oil, wheat germ oil, coconut oil, flaxseed oil, almond oil, safflower oil, etc.*

Animal Hair.
In some blankets, mattresses, brushes, furniture, etc. *Alternatives: vegetable and synthetic fibers.*

Arachidonic Acid.
A liquid unsaturated fatty acid that is found in liver, brain, glands, and fat of animals and humans. Generally isolated from animal liver. Used in companion animal food for nutrition and in skin creams and lotions to soothe eczema and rashes. *Alternatives: synthetics, aloe vera, tea tree oil, calendula ointment.*

Arachidyl Proprionate.
A wax that can be from animal fat. *Alternatives: peanut or vegetable oil.*

Aspartic Acid. Aminosuccinate Acid.
Can be animal or plant source (e.g., molasses). Sometimes synthesized for commercial purposes.

Bee Pollen.
Microsporic grains in seed plants gathered by bees, then collected from the legs of bees. Causes allergic reactions in some people. In nutritional supplements, shampoos, toothpastes, deodorants. *Alternatives: synthetics, plant amino acids, pollen collected from plants.*

Bee Products.
Produced by bees for their own use. Bees are selectively bred. Culled bees are killed. A cheap sugar is substituted for their stolen honey. Millions die as a result. Their legs are often torn off by pollen-collection trapdoors.

Beeswax. Honeycomb.
Wax obtained from melting honeycomb with boiling water, straining it, and cooling it. From virgin bees. Very cheap and widely used but harmful to the skin. In lipsticks and many other cosmetics (especially face creams, lotions, mascara, eye creams and shadows, face makeups, nail whiteners, lip balms, etc.). Derivatives: **Cera Flava**. *Alternatives: paraffin, vegetable oils and fats. Ceresin, aka ceresine, aka earth wax. (Made from the mineral ozokerite. Replaces beeswax in cosmetics. Also used to wax paper, to make polishing cloths, in dentistry for taking wax impressions, and in candle-making.) Also, carnauba wax (from the Brazilian palm tree; used in many cosmetics, including lipstick; rarely causes allergic reactions). Candelilla wax (from candelilla plants; used in many cosmetics, including lipstick; also in the manufacture of rubber and phonograph records, in waterproofing and writing inks; no known toxicity). Japan wax (Vegetable wax. Japan tallow. Fat from the fruit of a tree grown in Japan and China.).*

Benzoic Acid.
In almost all vertebrates and in berries. Used as a preservative in mouthwashes, deodorants, creams, aftershave lotions, etc. *Alternatives: cranberries, gum benzoin (tincture) from the aromatic balsamic resin from trees grown in China, Sumatra, Thailand, and Cambodia.*

Beta Carotene.
(See **Carotene**.)

Biotin. Vitamin H. Vitamin B Factor.
In every living cell and in larger amounts in milk and yeast. Used as a texturizer in cosmetics, shampoos, and creams. *Alternatives: plant sources.*

Blood.
From any slaughtered animal. Used as adhesive in plywood, also found in cheese-making, foam rubber, intravenous feedings, and medicines. Possibly in foods such as lecithin. *Alternatives: synthetics, plant sources.*

Boar Bristles.
Hair from wild or captive hogs. In "natural" toothbrushes and bath and shaving brushes. *Alternatives: vegetable fibers, nylon, the peelu branch or peelu gum (Asian, available in the U.S.; its juice replaces toothpaste).*

Bone Char.
Animal bone ash. Used in bone china and often to make sugar white. Serves as the charcoal used in aquarium filters. *Alternatives: synthetic tribasic calcium phosphate.*

Bone Meal.
Crushed or ground animal bones. In some fertilizers. In some vitamins and supplements as a source of calcium. In toothpastes. *Alternatives: plant mulch, vegetable compost, dolomite, clay, vegetarian vitamins.*

Calciferol.
(See **Vitamin D**.)

Calfskin.
(See **Leather**.)

Caprylamine Oxide.
(See **Caprylic Acid**.)

Capryl Betaine.
(See **Caprylic Acid**.)

Caprylic Acid.
A liquid fatty acid from cow's or goat's milk. Also from palm and coconut oil, other plant oils. In perfumes, soaps. Derivatives: **Caprylic Triglyceride, Caprylamine Oxide, Capryl Betaine**. *Alternatives: plant sources.*

Caprylic Triglyceride.
(See **Caprylic Acid**.)

Carbamide.
(See **Urea**.)

Carmine. Cochineal. Carminic Acid.
Red pigment from the crushed female cochineal insect. Reportedly, 70,000 beetles must be killed to produce one pound of this red dye. Used in cosmetics, shampoos, red applesauce, and other foods (including red lollipops and food coloring). May cause allergic reaction. *Alternatives: beet juice (used in powders, rouges, shampoos; no known toxicity); alkanet root (from the root of this herb-like tree; used as a red dye for inks, wines, lip balms, etc.; no known toxicity. Can also be combined to make a copper or blue coloring). (See **Colors**.)*

Carminic Acid.
(See **Carmine**.)

Carotene. Provitamin A. Beta Carotene.
A pigment found in many animal tissues and in all plants. Used as a coloring in cosmetics and in the manufacture of vitamin A.

Casein. Caseinate. Sodium Caseinate.
Milk protein. In "nondairy" creamers, soy cheese, many cosmetics, hair preparations, beauty masks. *Alternatives: soy protein, soy milk, and other vegetable milks.*

Caseinate.
(See **Casein**.)

Cashmere.
Wool from the Kashmir goat. Used in clothing. *Alternatives: synthetic fibers.*

Castor. Castoreum.
Creamy substance with strong odor from muskrat and beaver genitals. Used as a fixative in perfume and incense. *Alternatives: synthetics, plant castor oil.*

Castoreum.
(See **Castor**.)

Catgut.
Tough string from the intestines of sheep, horses, etc. Used for surgical sutures. Also for stringing tennis rackets and musical instruments, etc. *Alternatives: nylon and other synthetic fibers.*

Cera Flava.
(See **Beeswax**.)

Cerebrosides.
Fatty acids and sugars found in the covering of nerves. May include tissue from brains.

Cetyl Alcohol.
Wax found in spermaceti from sperm whales or dolphins. *Alternatives: vegetable cetyl alcohol (e.g., coconut), synthetic spermaceti.*

Cetyl Palmitate.
(See **Spermaceti**.)

Chitosan.
A fiber derived from crustacean shells. Used as a lipid binder in diet products, in hair, oral, and skin care products, antiperspirants, and deodorants. *Alternatives: raspberries, yams, legumes, dried apricots, and many other fruits and vegetables.*

Cholesterin.
(See **Lanolin**.)

Cholesterol.
A steroid alcohol in all animal fats and oils, nervous tissue, egg yolk, and blood. Can be derived from lanolin. In cosmetics, eye creams, shampoos, etc. *Alternatives: solid complex alcohols (sterols) from plant sources.*

Choline Bitartrate.
(See **Lecithin**.)

Civet.
Unctuous secretion painfully scraped from a gland very near the genital organs of civet cats. Used as a fixative in perfumes. *Alternatives: (See alternatives to **Musk**).*

Cochineal.
(See **Carmine**.)

Cod Liver Oil.
(See **Marine Oil**.)

Collagen.
Fibrous protein in vertebrates. Usually derived from animal tissue. Can't affect the skin's own collagen. An allergen. *Alternatives: soy protein, almond oil, amla oil (see alternatives to **Keratin**), etc.*

Colors. Dyes.
Pigments from animal, plant, and synthetic sources used to color foods, cosmetics, and other products. Cochineal is from insects. Widely used FD&C and D&C colors are coal-tar (bituminous coal) derivatives that are continuously tested on animals due to their carcinogenic properties. *Alternatives: grapes, beets, turmeric, saffron, carrots, chlorophyll, annatto, alkanet.*

Corticosteroid.
(See **Cortisone**.)

Cortisone. Corticosteroid.
Hormone from adrenal glands. Widely used in medicine. *Alternatives: synthetics.*

Cysteine, L-Form.
An amino acid from hair, often obtained from animals. Used in hair-care products and creams, in some bakery products, and in wound-healing formulations. *Alternatives: plant sources.*

Cystine.
An amino acid found in urine and horsehair. Used as a nutritional supplement and in emollients. *Alternatives: plant sources.*

Dexpanthenol.
(See **Panthenol**.)

Diglycerides.
(See **Monoglycerides** and **Glycerin**.)

Dimethyl Stearamine.
(See **Stearic Acid**.)

Down.
Goose or duck insulating feathers. From slaughtered or cruelly exploited geese. Used as an insulator in quilts, parkas, sleeping bags, pillows, etc. *Alternatives: polyester and synthetic substitutes, kapok (silky fibers from the seeds of some tropical trees) and milkweed seed pod fibers.*

Duodenum Substances.
From the digestive tracts of cows and pigs. Added to some vitamin tablets. In some medicines. *Alternatives: vegetarian vitamins, synthetics.*

Dyes.
(See **Colors**.)

Egg Protein.
In shampoos, skin preparations, etc. *Alternatives: plant proteins.*

Elastin.
Protein found in the neck ligaments and aortas of cows. Similar to collagen. Can't affect the skin's own elasticity. *Alternatives: synthetics, protein from plant tissues.*

Emu Oil.
From flightless ratite birds native to Australia and now factory farmed. Used in cosmetics and creams. *Alternatives: vegetable and plant oils.*

Ergocalciferol.
(See **Vitamin D**.)

Ergosterol.
(See **Vitamin D**.)

Estradiol.
(See **Estrogen**.)

Estrogen. Estradiol.
Female hormones from pregnant mares' urine. Considered a drug. Can have harmful systemic effects if used by children. Used for reproductive problems and in birth control pills and Premarin, a menopausal drug. In creams, perfumes, and lotions. Has a negligible effect in the creams as a skin restorative; simple vegetable-source emollients are considered better. *Alternatives: oral contraceptives and menopausal drugs based on synthetic steroids or phytoestrogens (from plants, especially palm-kernel oil). Menopausal symptoms can also be treated with diet and herbs.*

Fats.
(See **Animal Fats**.)

Fatty Acids.
Can be one or any mixture of liquid and solid acids such as caprylic, lauric, myristic, oleic, palmitic, and stearic. Used in bubble baths, lipsticks, soap, detergents, cosmetics, food. *Alternatives: vegetable-derived acids, soy lecithin, safflower oil, bitter almond oil, sunflower oil, etc.*

FD&C Colors.
(See **Colors**.)

Feathers.
From exploited and slaughtered birds. Used whole as ornaments or ground up in shampoos. (See **Down** and **Keratin**.)

Fish Liver Oil.
Used in vitamins and supplements. In milk fortified with vitamin D. *Alternatives: yeast extract ergosterol and exposure of skin to sunshine.*

Fish Oil.
(See **Marine Oil**.) Fish oil can also be from marine mammals. Used in soap-making.

Fish Scales.
Used in shimmery makeups. *Alternatives: mica, rayon, synthetic pearl.*

Fur.
Obtained from animals (usually mink, foxes, or rabbits) cruelly trapped in steel-jaw leghold traps or raised in intensive confinement on fur "farms." *Alternatives: synthetics.* (See **Sable Brushes**.)

Gel.
(See **Gelatin**.)

Gelatin. Gel.
Protein obtained by boiling skin, tendons, ligaments, and/or bones with water. From cows and pigs. Used in shampoos, face masks, and other cosmetics. Used as a thickener for fruit gelatins and puddings (e.g., "Jello"). In candies, marshmallows, cakes, ice cream, yogurts. On photographic film and in vitamins as a coating and as capsules. Sometimes used to assist in "clearing" wines. *Alternatives: carrageen (carrageenan, Irish moss), seaweeds (algin, agar-agar, kelp—used in jellies, plastics, medicine), pectin from fruits, dextrins, locust bean gum, cotton gum, silica gel. Marshmallows were originally made from the root of the marsh mallow plant. Vegetarian capsules are now available from several companies. Digital cameras don't use film.*

Glucose Tyrosinase.
(See **Tyrosine**.)

Glycerides.
(See **Glycerin**.)

Glycerin. Glycerol.
A byproduct of soap manufacture (normally uses animal fat). In cosmetics, foods, mouthwashes, chewing gum, toothpastes, soaps, ointments, medicines, lubricants, transmission and brake fluid, and plastics. Derivatives: **Glycerides, Glyceryls, Glycreth-26, Polyglycerol.** *Alternatives: vegetable glycerin—a byproduct of vegetable oil soap. Derivatives of seaweed, petroleum.*

Glycerol.
(See **Glycerin.**)

Glyceryls.
(See **Glycerin.**)

Glycreth-26.
(See **Glycerin.**)

Guanine. Pearl Essence.
Obtained from scales of fish. Constituent of ribonucleic acid and deoxyribonucleic acid and found in all animal and plant tissues. In shampoo, nail polish, other cosmetics. *Alternatives: leguminous plants, synthetic pearl, or aluminum and bronze particles.*

Hide Glue.
Same as gelatin but of a cruder impure form. *Alternatives: dextrins and synthetic petrochemical-based adhesives.* (See **Gelatin.**)

Honey.
Food for bees, made by bees. Can cause allergic reactions. Used as a coloring and an emollient in cosmetics and as a flavoring in foods. Should never be fed to infants. *Alternatives: in foods—maple syrup, date sugar, syrups made from grains such as barley malt, turbinado sugar, molasses; in cosmetics—vegetable colors and oils.*

Honeycomb.
(See **Beeswax.**)

Horsehair.
(See **Animal Hair.**)

Hyaluronic Acid.
A protein found in umbilical cords and the fluids around the joints. Used in cosmetics. *Alternatives: plant oils.*

Hydrocortisone.
(See **Cortisone.**)

Hydrolyzed Animal Protein.
In cosmetics, especially shampoo and hair treatments. *Alternatives: soy protein, other vegetable proteins, amla oil (see alternatives to **Keratin**).*

Imidazolidinyl Urea.
(See **Urea.**)

Insulin.
From hog pancreas. Used by millions of diabetics daily. *Alternatives: synthetics, vegetarian diet and nutritional supplements, human insulin grown in a lab.*

Isinglass.
A form of gelatin prepared from the internal membranes of fish bladders. Sometimes used in "clearing" wines and in foods. *Alternatives: bentonite clay, "Japanese isinglass," agar-agar (see alternatives to **Gelatin**), mica, a mineral used in cosmetics.*

Isopropyl Lanolate.
(See **Lanolin**.)

Isopropyl Myristate.
(See **Myristic Acid**.)

Isopropyl Palmitate.
Complex mixtures of isomers of stearic acid and palmitic acid. (See **Stearic Acid**.)

Keratin.
Protein from the ground-up horns, hooves, feathers, quills, and hair of various animals. In hair rinses, shampoos, permanent wave solutions. *Alternatives: almond oil, soy protein, amla oil (from the fruit of an Indian tree), human hair from salons. Rosemary and nettle give body and strand strength to hair.*

Lactic Acid.
Found in blood and muscle tissue. Also in sour milk, beer, sauerkraut, pickles, and other food products made by bacterial fermentation. Used in skin fresheners, as a preservative, in the formation of plasticizers, etc. *Alternatives: plant milk sugars, synthetics.*

Lactose.
Milk sugar from milk of mammals. In eye lotions, foods, tablets, cosmetics, baked goods, medicines. *Alternatives: plant milk sugars.*

Laneth.
(See **Lanolin**.)

Lanogene.
(See **Lanolin**.)

Lanolin. Lanolin Acids. Wool Fat. Wool Wax.
A product of the oil glands of sheep, extracted from their wool. Used as an emollient in many skin care products and cosmetics and in medicines. An allergen with no proven effectiveness. (See **Wool** for cruelty to sheep.) Derivatives: **Aliphatic Alcohols, Cholesterin, Isopropyl Lanolate, Laneth, Lanogene, Lanolin Alcohols, Lanosterols, Sterols, Triterpene Alcohols.** *Alternatives: plant and vegetable oils.*

Lanolin Alcohol.
(See **Lanolin**.)

Lanosterols.
(See **Lanolin**.)

Lard.
Fat from hog abdomens. In shaving creams, soaps, cosmetics. In baked goods, French fries, refried beans, and many other foods. *Alternatives: pure vegetable fats or oils.*

Leather. Suede. Calfskin. Sheepskin. Alligator Skin. Other Types of Skin.
Subsidizes the meat industry. Used to make wallets, handbags, furniture and car upholstery, shoes, etc. *Alternatives: cotton, canvas, nylon, vinyl, ultrasuede, pleather, other synthetics.*

Lecithin. Choline Bitartrate.
Waxy substance in nervous tissue of all living organisms. But frequently obtained for commercial purposes from eggs and soybeans. Also from nerve tissue, blood, milk, corn. Choline bitartrate, the basic constituent of lecithin, is in many animal and plant tissues and prepared synthetically. Lecithin can be in eye creams, lipsticks, liquid powders, hand creams, lotions, soaps, shampoos, other cosmetics, and some medicines. *Alternatives: soybean lecithin, synthetics.*

Linoleic Acid.
An essential fatty acid. Used in cosmetics, vitamins. *Alternatives: (See alternatives to **Fatty Acids**.)*

Lipase.
Enzyme from the stomachs and tongue glands of calves, kids, and lambs. Used in cheese-making and in digestive aids. *Alternatives: vegetable enzymes, castor beans.*

Lipids.
(See **Lipoids**.)

Lipoids. Lipids.
Fat and fat-like substances that are found in animals and plants. *Alternatives: vegetable oils.*

Marine Oil.
From fish or marine mammals (including porpoises). Used in soap-making. Used as a shortening (especially in some margarines), as a lubricant, and in paint. *Alternatives: vegetable oils.*

Methionine.
Essential amino acid found in various proteins (usually from egg albumen and casein). Used as a texturizer and for freshness in potato chips. *Alternatives: synthetics.*

Milk Protein.
Hydrolyzed milk protein. From the milk of cows. In cosmetics, shampoos, moisturizers, conditioners, etc. *Alternatives: soy protein, other plant proteins.*

Mink Oil.
From minks. In cosmetics, creams, etc. *Alternatives: vegetable oils and emollients such as avocado oil, almond oil, and jojoba oil.*

Monoglycerides. Glycerides. (See Glycerin.)
From animal fat. In margarines, cake mixes, candies, foods, etc. In cosmetics. *Alternative: vegetable glycerides.*

Musk (Oil).
Dried secretion painfully obtained from musk deer, beaver, muskrat, civet cat, and otter genitals. Wild cats are kept captive in cages in horrible conditions and are whipped around the genitals to produce the scent; beavers are trapped; deer are shot. In perfumes and in food flavorings. *Alternatives: labdanum oil (which comes from various rockrose shrubs) and other plants with a musky scent. Labdanum oil has no known toxicity.*

Myristal Ether Sulfate.
(See **Myristic Acid.**)

Myristic Acid.
Organic acid in most animal and vegetable fats. In butter acids. Used in shampoos, creams, cosmetics. In food flavorings. Derivatives: **Isopropyl Myristate, Myristal Ether Sulfate, Myristyls, Oleyl Myristate.** *Alternatives: nut butters, oil of lovage, coconut oil, extract from seed kernels of nutmeg, etc.*

Myristyls.
(See **Myristic Acid.**)

"Natural Sources."
Can mean animal or vegetable sources. Most often in the health food industry, especially in the cosmetics area, it means animal sources, such as animal elastin, glands, fat, protein, and oil. *Alternatives: plant sources.*

Nucleic Acids.
In the nucleus of all living cells. Used in cosmetics, shampoos, conditioners, etc. Also in vitamins, supplements. *Alternatives: plant sources.*

Ocenol.
(See **Oleyl Alcohol.**)

Octyl Dodecanol.
Mixture of solid waxy alcohols. Primarily from stearyl alcohol. (See **Stearyl Alcohol.**)

Oils.
(See alternatives to **Animal Fats and Oils.**)

Oleic Acid.
Obtained from various animal and vegetable fats and oils. Usually obtained commercially from inedible tallow. (See **Tallow.**) In foods, soft soap, bar soap, permanent wave solutions, creams, nail polish, lipsticks, many other skin preparations. Derivatives: **Oleyl Oleate, Oleyl Stearate.** *Alternatives: coconut oil. (See alternatives to **Animal Fats and Oils.**)*

Oleths.
(See **Oleyl Alcohol.**)

Oleyl Alcohol. Ocenol.
Found in fish oils. Used in the manufacture of detergents, as a plasticizer for softening fabrics, and as a carrier for medications. Derivatives: **Oleths, Oleyl Arachidate, Oleyl Imidazoline.**

Oleyl Arachidate.
(See **Oleyl Alcohol**.)

Oleyl Imidazoline.
(See **Oleyl Alcohol**.)

Oleyl Myristate.
(See **Myristic Acid**.)

Oleyl Oleate.
(See **Oleic Acid**.)

Oleyl Stearate.
(See **Oleic Acid**.)

Palmitamide.
(See **Palmitic Acid**.)

Palmitamine.
(See **Palmitic Acid**.)

Palmitate.
(See **Palmitic Acid**.)

Palmitic Acid.
From fats, oils (see **Fatty Acids**). Mixed with stearic acid. Found in many animal fats and plant oils. In shampoos, shaving soaps, creams. Derivatives: **Palmitate**, **Palmitamine**, **Palmitamide**. *Alternatives: palm oil, vegetable sources.*

Panthenol. Dexpanthenol. Vitamin B-Complex Factor. Provitamin B-5.
Can come from animal or plant sources or synthetics. In shampoos, supplements, emollients, etc. In foods. Derivative: **Panthenyl**. *Alternatives: synthetics, plants.*

Panthenyl.
(See **Panthenol**.)

Pepsin.
In hogs' stomachs. A clotting agent. In some cheeses and vitamins. Same uses and alternatives as **Rennet**.

Placenta. Placenta Polypeptides Protein. Afterbirth.
Contains waste matter eliminated by the fetus. Derived from the uterus of slaughtered animals. Animal placenta is widely used in skin creams, shampoos, masks, etc. *Alternatives: kelp. (See alternatives to **Animal Fats and Oils**.)*

Polyglycerol.
(See **Glycerin**.)

Polypeptides.
From animal protein. Used in cosmetics. *Alternatives: plant proteins and enzymes.*

Polysorbates.
Derivatives of fatty acids. In cosmetics, foods.

Pristane.
Obtained from the liver oil of sharks and from whale ambergris. (See **Squalene, Ambergris.**) Used as a lubricant and anti-corrosive agent. In cosmetics. *Alternatives: plant oils, synthetics.*

Progesterone.
A steroid hormone used in anti-wrinkle face creams. Can have adverse systemic effects. *Alternatives: synthetics.*

Propolis.
Tree sap gathered by bees and used as a sealant in beehives. In toothpaste, shampoo, deodorant, supplements, etc. *Alternatives: tree sap, synthetics.*

Provitamin A.
(See **Carotene**.)

Provitamin B-5.
(See **Panthenol**.)

Provitamin D-2.
(See **Vitamin D**.)

Rennet. Rennin.
Enzyme from calves' stomachs. Used in cheese-making, rennet custard (junket), and in many coagulated dairy products. *Alternatives: microbial coagulating agents, bacteria culture, lemon juice, or vegetable rennet.*

Rennin.
(See **Rennet**.)

Resinous Glaze.
(See **Shellac**.)

Ribonucleic Acid.
(See **RNA**.)

RNA. Ribonucleic Acid.
RNA is in all living cells. Used in many protein shampoos and cosmetics. *Alternatives: plant cells.*

Royal Jelly.
Secretion from the throat glands of the honeybee workers that is fed to the larvae in a colony and to all queen larvae. No proven value in cosmetics preparations. *Alternatives: aloe vera, comfrey, other plant derivatives.*

Sable Brushes.
From the fur of sables (weasel-like mammals). Used to make eye makeup, lipstick, and artists' brushes. *Alternatives: synthetic fibers.*

Sea Turtle Oil.
(See **Turtle Oil.**)

Shark Liver Oil.
Used in lubricating creams and lotions. Derivatives: **Squalane, Squalene.** *Alternatives: vegetable oils.*

Sheepskin.
(See **Leather.**)

Shellac. Resinous Glaze.
Resinous excretion of certain insects. Used as a candy glaze, in hair lacquer, and on jewelry. *Alternatives: plant waxes.*

Silk. Silk Powder.
Silk is the shiny fiber made by silkworms to form their cocoons. Worms are boiled in their cocoons to get the silk. Used in cloth. In silk-screening (other fine cloth can be and is used instead). Taffeta can be made from silk or nylon. Silk powder is obtained from the secretion of the silkworm. It is used as a coloring agent in face powders, soaps, etc. Can cause severe allergic skin reactions and systemic reactions (if inhaled or ingested). *Alternatives: milkweed seed-pod fibers, nylon, silk-cotton tree and ceiba tree filaments (kapok), rayon, and synthetic silks.*

Snails.
In some cosmetics (crushed).

Sodium Caseinate.
(See **Casein.**)

Sodium Steroyl Lactylate.
(See **Lactic Acid.**)

Sodium Tallowate.
(See **Tallow.**)

Spermaceti. Cetyl Palmitate. Sperm Oil.
Waxy oil derived from the sperm whale's head or from dolphins. In many margarines. In skin creams, ointments, shampoos, candles, etc. Used in the leather industry. May become rancid and cause irritations. *Alternatives: synthetic spermaceti, jojoba oil, and other vegetable emollients.*

Sponge (Luna and Sea).
A plant-like animal. Lives in the sea. Becoming scarce. *Alternatives: synthetic sponges, loofahs (plants used as sponges).*

Squalane.
(See **Shark Liver Oil.**)

Squalene.
Oil from shark livers, etc. In cosmetics, moisturizers, hair dyes, surface-active agents. *Alternatives: vegetable emollients such as olive oil, wheat germ oil, rice bran oil, etc.*

Stearamide.
(See **Stearic Acid**.)

Stearamine.
(See **Stearic Acid**.)

Stearamine Oxide.
(See **Stearyl Alcohol**.)

Stearates.
(See **Stearic Acid**.)

Stearic Acid.
Fat from cows and sheep and from dogs and cats euthanized in animal shelters, etc. Most often refers to a fatty substance taken from the stomachs of pigs. Can be harsh, irritating. Used in cosmetics, soaps, lubricants, candles, hairspray, conditioners, deodorants, creams, chewing gum, food flavoring. Derivatives: **Stearamide, Stearamine, Stearates, Stearic Hydrazide, Stearone, Stearoxytrimethylsilane, Stearoyl Lactylic Acid, Stearyl Betaine, Stearyl Imidazoline.** *Alternatives: Stearic acid can be found in many vegetable fats and coconut.*

Stearic Hydrazide.
(See **Stearic Acid**.)

Stearone.
(See **Stearic Acid**.)

Stearoxytrimethylsilane.
(See **Stearic Acid**.)

Stearoyl Lactylic Acid.
(See **Stearic Acid**.)

Stearyl Acetate.
(See **Stearyl Alcohol**.)

Stearyl Alcohol. Sterols.
A mixture of solid alcohols. Can be prepared from sperm whale oil. In medicines, creams, rinses, shampoos, etc. Derivatives: **Stearamine Oxide, Stearyl Acetate, Stearyl Caprylate, Stearyl Citrate, Stearyldimethyl Amine, Stearyl Glycyrrhetinate, Stearyl Heptanoate, Stearyl Octanoate, Stearyl Stearate.** *Alternatives: plant sources, vegetable stearic acid.*

Stearyl Betaine.
(See **Stearic Acid**.)

Stearyl Caprylate.
(See **Stearyl Alcohol**.)

Stearyl Citrate.
(See **Stearyl Alcohol**.)

Stearyldimethyl Amine.
(See **Stearyl Alcohol**.)

Stearyl Glycyrrhetinate.
(See **Stearyl Alcohol**.)

Stearyl Heptanoate.
(See **Stearyl Alcohol**.)

Stearyl Imidazoline.
(See **Stearic Acid**.)

Stearyl Octanoate.
(See **Stearyl Alcohol**.)

Stearyl Stearate.
(See **Stearyl Alcohol**.)

Steroids. Sterols.
From various animal glands or from plant tissues. Steroids include sterols. Sterols are alcohol from animals or plants (e.g., cholesterol). Used in hormone preparation. In creams, lotions, hair conditioners, fragrances, etc. *Alternatives: plant tissues, synthetics.*

Sterols.
(See **Stearyl Alcohol** and **Steroids**.)

Suede.
(See **Leather**.)

Tallow. Tallow Fatty Alcohol. Stearic Acid.
Rendered beef fat. May cause eczema and blackheads. In wax paper, crayons, margarines, paints, rubber, lubricants, etc. In candles, soaps, lipsticks, shaving creams, other cosmetics. Chemicals (e.g., PCB) can be in animal tallow. Derivatives: **Sodium Tallowate**, **Tallow Acid**, **Tallow Amide**, **Tallow Amine**, **Talloweth-6**, **Tallow Glycerides**, **Tallow Imidazoline**. *Alternatives: vegetable tallow, Japan tallow, paraffin, and/or ceresin (see alternatives to* **Beeswax** *for all three). Paraffin is usually from petroleum, wood, coal, or shale oil.*

Tallow Acid.
(See **Tallow**.)

Tallow Amide.
(See **Tallow**.)

Tallow Amine.
(See **Tallow**.)

Talloweth-6.
(See **Tallow**.)

Tallow Glycerides.
(See **Tallow**.)

Tallow Imidazoline.
(See **Tallow**.)

Triterpene Alcohols.
(See **Lanolin**.)

Turtle Oil. Sea Turtle Oil.
From the muscles and genitals of giant sea turtles. In soap, skin creams, nail creams, other cosmetics. *Alternatives: vegetable emollients (see alternatives to **Animal Fats and Oils**).*

Tyrosine.
Amino acid hydrolyzed from casein. Used in cosmetics and creams. Derivative: **Glucose Tyrosinase**.

Urea. Carbamide.
Excreted from urine and other bodily fluids. In deodorants, ammoniated dentifrices, mouthwashes, hair colorings, hand creams, lotions, shampoos, etc. Used to "brown" baked goods, such as pretzels. Derivatives: **Imidazolidinyl Urea**, **Uric Acid**. *Alternatives: synthetics.*

Uric Acid.
(See **Urea**.)

Vitamin A.
Can come from fish liver oil (e.g., shark liver oil), egg yolk, butter, lemongrass, wheat germ oil, carotene in carrots, and synthetics. It is an aliphatic alcohol. In cosmetics, creams, perfumes, hair dyes, etc. In vitamins, supplements. *Alternatives: carrots, other vegetables, synthetics.*

Vitamin B-Complex Factor.
(See **Panthenol**.)

Vitamin B Factor.
(See **Biotin**.)

Vitamin B-12.
Usually animal source. Some vegetarian B-12 vitamins are in a stomach base. *Alternatives: Some vegetarian B-12-fortified yeasts and analogs available. Plant algae discovered containing B-12, now in supplement form (spirulina). Some nutritionists caution that fortified foods or supplements are essential.*

Vitamin D. Ergocalciferol. Vitamin D-2. Ergosterol. Provitamin D-2. Calciferol. Vitamin D-3.
Vitamin D can come from fish liver oil, milk, egg yolk, etc. Vitamin D-2 can come from animal fats or plant sterols. Vitamin D-3 is always from an animal source. All the D vitamins can be in creams, lotions, other cosmetics, vitamin tablets, etc. *Alternatives: plant and mineral sources, synthetics, completely vegetarian vitamins, exposure of skin to sunshine. Many other vitamins can come from animal sources. Examples: choline, biotin, inositol, riboflavin, etc.*

Vitamin H.
(See **Biotin**.)

Wax.
Glossy, hard substance that is soft when hot. From animals and plants. In lipsticks, depilatories, hair straighteners. *Alternatives: vegetable waxes.*

Whey.
A serum from milk. Usually in cakes, cookies, candies, and breads. In cheese-making. *Alternatives: soybean whey.*

Wool.
From sheep. Used in clothing. Ram lambs and old "wool" sheep are slaughtered for their meat. Sheep are transported without food or water, in extreme heat and cold. Legs are broken, eyes injured, etc. Sheep are bred to be unnaturally woolly, also unnaturally wrinkly, which causes them to get insect infestations around the tail areas. The farmer's solution to this is the painful cutting away of the flesh around the tail (called "mulesing"). "Inferior" sheep are killed. When shearing the sheep, they are pinned down violently and sheared roughly. Their skin is cut up. Every year, hundreds of thousands of shorn sheep die from exposure to cold. Natural predators of sheep (wolves, coyotes, eagles, etc.) are poisoned, trapped, and shot. In the U.S., overgrazing of cattle and sheep is turning more than 150 million acres of land to desert. "Natural" wool production uses enormous amounts of resources and energy (to breed, raise, feed, shear, transport, slaughter, etc., the sheep). Derivatives: **Lanolin, Wool Wax, Wool Fat.** *Alternatives: cotton, cotton flannel, synthetic fibers, ramie, etc.*

Wool Fat.
(See **Lanolin.**)

Wool Wax.
(See **Lanolin.**)

REFERENCES
Buyukmihci, Nermin. "John Cardillo's List of Animal Products and Their Alternatives."
Cosmetic Ingredients Glossary: A Basic Guide to Natural Body Care Products. Petaluma, Calif.: Feather River Co., 1988.
Mason, Jim, and Peter Singer. *Animal Factories.* New York: Crown Publishers, Inc., 1980.
Ruesch, Hans. *Slaughter of the Innocent.* New York: Civitas, 1983.
Singer, Peter. *Animal Liberation.* New York: Random House, 1990.
Sweethardt Herb Catalogue.
Webster's Third New International Dictionary. Springfield, Mass.: Merriam-Webster Inc., 1981.
Winter, Ruth. *A Consumer's Dictionary of Cosmetic Ingredients.* New York: Crown Publishing Group, 1994.
Winter, Ruth. *A Consumer's Dictionary of Food Additives.* New York: Crown Publishing Group, 1994.

ALTERNATIVES TO LEATHER AND OTHER ANIMAL PRODUCTS

WHAT'S WRONG WITH LEATHER?

■ When you buy a leather jacket or leather shoes, you support animal suffering.

■ Millions of cows, pigs, sheep, and goats are slaughtered for their skin. They are castrated, branded, tail-docked, and dehorned without anesthesia. Then they are trucked to slaughter, bled to death, and skinned.

■ Leather isn't a slaughterhouse byproduct. The meat industry relies on skin sales to stay in business.

■ Animal skin is turned into finished leather through the use of dangerous mineral salts, formaldehyde, coal-tar derivatives, and cyanide-based oils and dyes.

■ People who have worked in or lived near tanneries are dying of cancer caused by exposure to toxic chemicals used to process and dye the leather. A New York State Department of Health study found that more than half of all testicular cancer victims work in tanneries.

Buying nonleather shoes, belts, wallets, bags—even baseballs—has never been easier. This section is divided into three parts: companies that sell only nonleather products, companies that carry some nonleather products, and an easy-to-use list of companies organized by type of product.

VEGAN COMPANIES

The following companies sell only animal-friendly and cruelty-free products. Most sell their products only through catalogs and online shopping sites, but some do sell their products through either their own retail store or other retail outlets.

Aesop, Inc.
P.O. Box 315, N. Cambridge, MA 02140
Tel.: 617-628-8030 • E-Mail: aesop@aesopinc.com
Web site: www.aesopinc.com
This company sells a wide variety of footwear, belts, wallets, and other nonleather items.

Ethical Wares
Caegwyn, Temple Bar, Felinfach, Lampeter, Ceredigion SA48 7SA Wales, U.K.
Tel.: 011 44 1570 741155 • E-Mail: vegans@ethicalwares.com
Web site: www.ethicalwares.com
This company carries shoe styles that include trekking and hiking boots, dress boots, steel-toe safety boots, and dress shoes for men and women.
🛒

Evolutionary Fur
Tel.: 800-FAKE-FUR
Web site: www.evolutionaryfur.com
Oleg Cassini designs this entirely vegan line of faux fur coats, complete with an anti-fur message on the label. Call for a retailer in your area.

Ex-tredz
388 Carlaw Ave., #100-D, Toronto, Ontario M4M 2T4 Canada
Tel.: 800-665-9182
Although this company doesn't sell directly to the public, consumers can call this number to find a local retailer that sells its products, which include vests, coats, belts, bags, etc., from recycled rubber.

Green Shoes
Station Rd., Totnes, Devon TQ9 5HW U.K.
Tel.: 011 44 180 386 4997
Order this company's catalog to find men's, women's, and children's shoes, boots, and casual sandals made-to-fit from nonleather materials.

Companies listed in this guide that are marked with a (🛒) are included in PETA's online shopping mall at wwwPETAMall.com.

Heartland Products, Ltd.
P.O. Box 218, Dakota City, IA 50529
Tel.: 800-441-4692 • Web site: www.trvnet.net/~hrtlndp/
Everything in the Heartland catalog is nonleather, from Western-style boots and baseball gloves to clogs, watchbands, and biker jackets.

NoBull Footwear
15 Chichester Dr. E., Saltdean, Brighton BN2 8LD U.K.
Tel./Fax: 011 44 1273 302979 • Web site: www.veganstore.co.uk
Sells a variety of high-quality vegan dress and casual shoes, hiking boots, jackets, belts, and wallets.

Pangea
7829 Woodmont Ave., Bethesda, MD 20814
Tel.: 301-652-3181 • E-Mail: pangeaveg@aol.com
Web site: www.pangeaveg.com
This mail-order company and store carries all cruelty-free, vegan products, including leather-alternative shoes, clothing, belts, and bags.

Planet Hemp
P.O. Box 424, Mount Morris, IL 64054
Tel.: 800-681-HEMP • E-Mail: sales@planethemp.com
Web site: www.planethemp.com
Planet Hemp's mail-order catalog offers hemp products such as women's and men's clothing, backpacks, sandals, wallets, and bags.

Planet V
43 Zoar St., Lower Gornal, Dudley, West Midlands DY3 2PA U.K.
Tel.: 011 44 138 425 2100 • E-Mail: sales@planetv.co.uk
Web site: www.planetv.co.uk
Planet V offers a full online catalog with shoes, boots, jackets, and coats.
☒

Tomorrow's World
9665 First View St., Norfolk, VA 23503
Tel.: 800-229-7571 • E-Mail: comments@tomorrowsworld.com
Web site: www.tomorrowsworld.com
This company distributes the entire Deja line through mail order. It carries nonleather clothing, shoes, belts, bags, etc., as well as organic hemp products.

Used Rubber USA
597 Haight St., San Francisco, CA 94117
Tel.: 415-626-7855 • E-Mail: info@usedrubberusa.com
Web site: www.usedrubberusa.com
Recycled rubber inner tubes and tires are used to make wallets, organizers, and bags in a variety of sizes. Please send $2 for a catalog.

Veganline
Freepost LON 10506, London SW14 1YY U.K.
E-Mail: nude@animal.nu • Web site: www.animal.nu
This company carries stylish vegan shoes, boots, and belts.

Vegan Wares
78 Smith St., Collingwood, 3066 VIC Australia
Tel.: 011 61 3 9417 0230 • E-Mail: veganw@veganwares.com
Web site: www.veganwares.com
This company offers nonleather shoes, boots, briefcases, wallets, dog collars, and ballet slippers.
☒

Vegetarian Shoes
12 Gardner St., Brighton, East Sussex BN1 1UP U.K.
Tel.: 011 44 127 369 1913 • E-Mail: information@vegetarian-shoes.co.uk
Web site: www.vegetarian-shoes.co.uk
This company carries more than 50 styles of synthetic leather and synthetic suede shoes, including genuine Doc Martens boots and shoes, Birkenstocks, dress shoes, hiking boots, work boots, "pleather" jackets, and belts.

OTHER COMPANIES SELLING LEATHER ALTERNATIVES

Active Soles
318 Court St., Plymouth, MA 02360
Tel.: 800-881-4322 • Web site: www.activesoles.com
This company distributes several styles of New Balance shoes, made from synthetic materials, for men and women.

Adidas
Tel.: 800-982-9337 • E-Mail: customerservice@thestore.adidas.com
Web site: www.adidas.com
Many styles of nonleather shoes are available through major retail outlets. Call for specific styles.

Aerostitch/Rider Warehouse
8 S. 18th Ave. W., Duluth, MN 55806
Tel.: 800-222-1994 • E-Mail: products@aerostitch.com
Web site: www.aerostitch.com
Nonleather cycling apparel.

Airwalk
603 Park Point Dr., Golden, CO 80401
Tel.: 303-526-2100 • E-Mail: joconnor@airwalk.com
Web site: www.airwalk.com
All snowboots from the 2000 line are produced from synthetic materials.

American Hemp and Earth Goods
Box 28185, Spokane, WA 99228
Tel.: 800-469-4367 • E-Mail: Info@ahbetterworld.com
Web site: www.ahbetterworld.com
Hemp wallets, bags, etc.

Anywear Shoes
55 S. Atlantic St., Seattle, WA 98134
Tel.: 888-425-0077 • E-Mail: sales@anywears.com
Web site: www.anywears.com
This company sells brightly colored, biodegradable, padded clogs that can be thrown in the washer.

Asics
16275 Laguna Canyon Rd., Irvine, CA 92618
Tel.: 800-678-9435 • E-Mail: consumer@asicstiger.com
Web site: www.asicstiger.com
Asics offers several synthetic shoes; call to find out about a specific shoe.

Avia
10200 S.W. Allen Blvd., Ste.1, Beaverton, OR 97005
Tel.: 800-345-2842 • E-Mail: service@aviashoes.com
Web site: www.aviashoes.com
535 Aerobics and 254 Running shoes are made from recycled synthetic materials.

Bakers Shoe Store
Weiss & Neuman Shoe Co.
2815 Scott Ave., St. Louis, MO 63103-1971
Tel.: 314-621-0699
This company offers vegan shoes for women.

Bata Shoe Company, Inc.
4501 Pulaski Hwy., Belcamp, MD 21017
Tel.: 800-365-2282 • Web site: www.bata.com
Bata manufactures industrial footwear and protective clothing. It offers nonleather high- and low-top boots suitable for factory or farm work.

Birkenstock Footwear
486 First St., Solvang, CA 93463
Tel.: 800-824-1228 • Web site: www.birkenstock.com
The Birki Too, Birki's, and Birki Kids lines of Birkenstocks are made of Birko-Flor synthetic uppers. For a totally animal-free shoe, ask for Birkolon synthetic footbed liners. Birki-Clogs are made entirely of polyurethane and a removable, washable footbed. Several styles of Birkenstocks and Betula come totally leather-free. For other styles, there is an extra charge to change the suede liner to a Birkolon liner.

Burton Snowboards
80 Industrial Pkwy., Burlington, VT 05401
Tel.: 800-881-3138 • E-Mail: info@burton.com
Web site: www.burton.com
Burton's Viking and Mystic-style boots are synthetic.

Capezio
One Campus Rd., Totowa, NJ 07512
Tel.: 800-234-4858 • Web site: www.capeziodance.com
626 Tapette for women and 626c Tapette for girls, as well as 625 Jr. Tyette for women and 625c Jr. Tyette for girls, are all synthetic.

Competition Accessories
345 Leffel Ln., Springfield, OH 45506
Tel.: 800-543-5141 • E-Mail: custservice@compacc.com
Web site: www.competitionaccessories.com
Nonleather cycling apparel.

Converse
Tel.: 800-428-2667 (U.S.)
    800-387-9550 (Canada)
Web site: www.converse.com
Chuck Taylor All-Stars, high-top and low-top, come in many styles, colors, and fabrics.

Daniel Green Company
One Main St., Dolgeville, NY 13329
Tel.: 800-342-2232 • E-Mail: sales@danielgreenco.com
Web site: www.danielgreenco.com
This company sells dressy leather-like sandals and flats.

DC Shoes
770 Sycamore Ave., #J471, Vista, CA 92083
Tel.: 760-599-2999 • E-Mail: info@dcshoes.com
Web Site: www.dcshoes.com
The Substance skateboarding shoe is 100 percent synthetic and is available in black, gray, navy, or white/navy.

Delia's
435 Hudson St., 3rd Fl., New York, NY 10014-3941
Tel.: 212-807-9060 • E-Mail: espeak@delias.com or custserv@delias.com
Web site: www.delias.com
A popular catalog geared to teenagers, with hip clothes and a good selection of vegan shoes.

Dennis Kirk
955 S. Field Ave., Rush City, MN 55069
Tel.: 800-328-9280 • E-Mail: info@denniskirk.com
Web site: www.denniskirk.com
Nonleather cycling apparel.

Dexter Shoes
71 Railroad Ave., Dexter, ME 04930
Tel.: 888-8-DEXTER • Web site: www.dexterbowling.com
Dexter Shoes carries several entirely synthetic styles of men's and women's bowling shoes.

Dr. Martens
Web site: www.drmartens.com
Boots, shoes, and clothing.

Ecolution
P.O. Box 2279, Merrifield, VA 22116
Tel.: 800-769-HEMP • E-Mail: orders@ecolution.com
Web site: www.ecolution.com
Purses, bags, and briefcases. Mail order.

Emerica
20161 Wind Row Dr., Wake Forest, CA 92630
Tel.: 949-460-2020 • Web site: www.emericaskate.com
A skateboarding shoe company that makes several vegan shoes.

Esprit
104 Challenger Dr., Portsmouth, TN 37148-1704
Tel.: 800-816-1535 • Web site: www.esprit.com
Clothing, shoes, bags, and purses.

Etnies
P.O. Box 1090, Lake Forest, CA 92630
Tel.: 949-460-2020 • Web site: www.etnies.com
The Etnies line includes two synthetic lines of skateboarding shoes: Vallely and Cyprus.

Etonic Shoes
Spalding Sports
425 Meadow St., Chicopee, MA 01021-0901
Tel.: 800-225-6601 • E-Mail: customer-relations@spalding.com
Web site: www.spalding.com
Etonic carries synthetic athletic shoes. Call for a store in your area.

Fabulous Furs
20 W. Pike St., Covington, KY 41011
Tel.: 606-291-3300 • E-Mail: custserv@fabulousfurs.com
Web site: www.fabulousfurs.com
This company sells exclusively faux fur coats.

Fila
14114 York Rd., Sparks, MD 21152
Tel.: 888-FILA-NET • E-Mail: fila@onlinestore.com
Web site: www.fila.com
Fila offers several synthetic shoes; call to find out about a specific shoe.

Five Ten
P.O. Box 1185, Redlands, CA 92373
Tel.: 909-798-4222 • Web site: www.spelean.com.au/FT/FiveTen.html
Five Ten's nonleather models of outdoor footwear include the VX, Anasazi Velcro, and
Anasazi Lace-Up.

Garmont, USA, Inc.
170 Boyer Cir., Williston, VT 05495
Tel.: 888-343-5200 • E-Mail: info@garmontusa.com
Web site: www.garmontusa.com
This company carries vegan hiking boots.

Heavenly Soles
615 W. Lake St., Minneapolis, MN 55408
Tel.: 612-822-2169 • E-Mail: shoes@ibm.net
Web site: www.heavenlysoles.com
Heavenly Soles offers shoes from Vegetarian Shoes.

Heelside Snowboarding
E-Mail: heelside99@aol.com • Web site: www.heelside.com
The Liftie, 50/50, and Explorer are synthetic.

J. Crew
One Ivy Crescent, Lynchburg, VA 24513
Tel.: 800-562-0258 • E-Mail: service@jcrew.com
Web site: www.jcrew.com
J. Crew's leather-alternative items include canvas deck shoes and basketball sneakers, nylon
sneakers, flannel deck sneakers, and rubber flip-flops and boots.

Keds
The Stride Rite Corporation
191 Spring St., Lexington, MA 02173
Tel.: 800-428-6575, ext. 2258 • E-Mail: keds@natcat.com
Web site: www.keds.com
Keds offers several synthetic shoes; call to find out about a specific shoe.

Kenneth Cole Reaction
152 W. 57th St., New York, NY 10019
Tel.: 877-REACTION • E-Mail: members@kcole.com
Web site: www.reaction.kencole.com
Another brand by Kenneth Cole. Many products are vegan.

LaCrosse Boots
1407 St. Andrew St., La Crosse, WI 54603
Tel.: 800-671-BOOT • Web site: www.lacrosse-outdoors.com
This company sells several styles of rubber boots: insulated, non-insulated, and steel toe, which are available from large retailers.

Lane Bryant
5 Limited Pkwy. E., Reynoldsburg, OH 43068
Tel.: 614-577-4000 • Web site: www.lanebryant.com
Lane Bryant's many stores carry synthetic pumps and sandals in a variety of styles.

The Last Resort
1014 Lake Ave., Lake Worth, FL 33460
Tel.: 561-586-4082 • E-Mail: urban@evcom.net
Web site: www.thelastresort.nu/shoes/Vegan/vegan.html
This company is a source for vegan Doc Martens boots and Creepers.
🛒

Life Stride
Brown Shoe
8300 Maryland Ave., St. Louis, MO 63105
Tel.: 314-854-4274 • E-Mail: info@brownshoe.com
Web site: www.browngroup.com/lifestride
This company sells synthetic pumps.

Madeline Stuart Shoes
Consolidated Shoe Company
10200 Timberlake Rd., Lynchburg, VA 24502
Tel.: 800-368-7463 • E-Mail: info@madelineshoes.com
Web site: www.madelineshoes.com
Offers a large line of fashionable women's shoes using linen, microfiber, and other synthetic materials.

Masseys
128 W. River St., Chippewa Falls, WI 54729
Tel.: 800-280-0846 • Web site: www.emasseys.com
Flats, pumps, and other shoes.

Nailers, Inc.
10845 Wheatland Ave., Ste. C, San Tee, CA 92071
Tel.: 619-562-2215
Nailers sells nonleather tool belts, nail bags, and kneepads, all made from Dupont's Cordura fabric.

Naturalizer
Tel.: 800-766-6465 • E-Mail: naturalizer@brownshoe.com
Web site: www.naturalizeronline.com
This company makes nonleather wedge pumps and snow boots.

New Balance
61 N. Beacon St., Boston, MA 02134
Web site: www.newbalance.com
New Balance carries a number of synthetic styles of athletic shoes.

Nike, Inc.
One Bowerman Dr., Beaverton, OR 97005
Tel.: 800-344-6453 • Web site: www.nikebiz.com
Call to receive a men's or women's sourcebook that lists all Nike shoes made with synthetic uppers. Nike also has synthetic children's and baby's shoes.

Nine West
1245 Forest Pkwy., West Deptford, NJ 08066-1728
Tel.: 800-999-1877 • Web site: www.ninewest.com
Shoes, belts, wallets, purses, bags, and other accessories.

Northwave
5000 First Ave. S., Seattle, WA 98134
Tel.: 206-762-2955 • E-Mail: nwtim@northwave.it
Web site: www.northwave.com
Stealth, Supercompact, and Team MTB cycling shoes are all synthetic.

Ohio Hempery Catalog
7002 State Rte. 329, Guysville, OH 45735
Tel.: 800-BUY-HEMP • E-Mail: hempery@hempery.com
Web site: www.hempery.com
This is a definitive source for hemp sandals, bags, purses, belts, wallets, and bike bags.

The OOOF Ball Company
454 W. Rose Tree Rd., Media, PA 19063
Tel.: 800-356-6631 • E-Mail: ooofball@aol.com
Web site: www.ooofball.com
This company sells nonleather medicine balls that bounce and float; for core body strength and conditioning to promote agility, endurance, flexibility, and balance; functional training for all sports; OOOF Ball games. Also offers books and videos.

Osiris
7130 Convoy Ct., San Diego, CA 92111
Web site: www.osirisshoes.com
Osiris carries many styles of vegan skateboarding shoes.

Payless Shoe Source
3231 S.E. Sixth St., Topeka, KS 66607
Tel.: 800-444-7463 • Web site: www.payless.com
This store has one of the widest selections of synthetic leather shoes available. The average store carries about 600 styles, 80 percent of which are synthetic. Leather shoes are marked on the box. Call for the location of a store in your area.

Perfect Image
307 Arbor Ridge Dr., Antioch, TN 37013
Tel.: 615-260-4520
This company designs faux fur accessories.

Prima Royale Shoes
5288 River Grade Rd., Irwindale, CA 91706
Tel.: 626-960-8388 • E-Mail: primashoes@aol.com
Mostly vegan shoes for women, sold in major department stores.

Reebok
1895 J.W. Foster Blvd., Canton, MA 02021
Tel.: 800-843-4444 • Web site: www.reebok.com
Reebok offers several synthetic shoes; call to find out about a specific shoe.

REI
1700 45th St. E., Sumner, WA 98390
Tel.: 800-426-4840 • Web site: www.rei.com
Adidas Adventure sandals, Teva sports sandals, Merrell sports sandals, and Nike sports sandals in nonleather styles are available. The company also offers nonleather belts and watchbands.

Road Runner Sports
5549 Copley Dr., San Diego, CA 92111
Tel.: 800-551-5558 • Web site: www.roadrunnersports.com
Nonleather running shoes include Brooks, Asics, New Balance, Saucony, Reebok, Mizuno, Adidas, and Etonic.

Roaman's
P.O. Box 8360, Indianapolis, IN 46283
Tel.: 800-274-7130
Roaman's carries several leather-like and canvas casual and dress shoes.

Sam & Libby
400 Technology Ct., Ste. F, Smyrna, GA 30082
Tel.: 770-801-1200 • E-Mail: info@samandlibby.com
Web site: samandlibby.com
Mostly vegan shoes for women, sold online and in major department stores.

Santana Canada Footwear
3770 Industrial Blvd., Sherbrooke, Quebec J1L 1N6 Canada
Tel.: 888-SANTANA
Waterproof nonleather boots and shoes are available in a variety of styles.

Saucony Inc.
13 Centennial Dr., Peabody, MA 01960
Tel.: 978-532-9000 • E-Mail: feedback@saucony.com
Web site: www.saucony.com
Saucony offers several synthetic shoes; call to find out about a specific shoe.

Skechers
P.O. Box 5060, Simi Valley, CA 93065
Tel.: 800-746-3411 • E-Mail: info@sketchers.com
Web site: www.sketchers.com
Sells in Skechers stores, through catalog, and online. Carries lots of canvas and rubbery shoes.

Soap Shoes
3109 Lomita Blvd., Torrance, CA 90505
Tel.: 310-643-1180 • E-Mail: grind@soapshoes.com
Web site: www.soapshoes.com
The company's Goa line is vegan.

Spalding Sports
425 Meadow St., Chicopee, MA 01021-0901
Tel.: 800-225-6601 • E-Mail: customer-relations@spalding.com
Web site: www.spalding.com
Spalding carries synthetic leather volleyballs, basketballs, softballs, soccer balls, and footballs. Call for a store in your area.

Steve Madden
52-16 Barnett Ave., Long Island City, NY 11104
Tel.: 888-SMADDEN • E-Mail: smdearsteve@worldnet.att.net
Web site: www.stevemadden.com
Offers many vegan women's shoes. Sells shoes in Steve Madden stores, in major department stores, and online.

Sunsports
P.O. Box 180, Stamford, CT 06904
Tel.: 800-308-HEMP
Hemp clothing, hats, and packs are available. The company also carries several styles of light shoes with hemp uppers.

Teva
P.O. Box 968, Flagstaff, AZ 86002
Tel.: 800-367-8382 • E-Mail: customerservice@tevasandals.com
Web site: www.teva.com
Sports shoes, sandals, and clothing.

Timberland
200 Domain Dr., Stratham, NH 03885
Tel.: 800-445-5545 • E-Mail: consumer_service@timberland.com
Web site: www.timberland.com
Shoes, clothing, outerwear, backpacks, and bags.

Tretorn
P.O. Box 3437, Boulder, CO 80307
Tel.: 800-525-2852 • E-Mail: info@tretornusa.com
Web site: www.tretorn.com
Tretorn specializes in canvas tennis-style shoes.

Unlisted by Kenneth Cole
3342 Melrose Ave., Roanoke, VA 24017
Tel.: 800-UNLISTED • Web site: www.kencole.com
This company offers a line of leather-like shoes, belts, and handbags for women. They are carried in some department stores. Call for locations near you.

Vans
15700 Shoemaker Ave., Santa Fe, CA 90670
Tel.: 800-750-VANS • E-Mail: custserv@vansshoes.com
Web site: www.vans.com
This company's nonleather styles include canvas, linen, and flannel Oxfords, mules, and Mary Janes.

V Sports
Tel.: 800-765-4200
Call to find out where synthetic soccer balls are sold in your area.

The Wet Seal, Inc.
26972 Burbank, Foothill Ranch, CA 92610
Tel.: 949-583-9029 • Web site: www.wetseal.com
No shoes sold online at the moment, but many of its stores sell vegan shoes. Geared toward teenage girls.

Wild Pair
Weiss and Neuman Shoe Co.
2815 Scott Ave., Ste. A, Saint Louis, MO 63103-1971
Tel.: 314-621-0699
Wild Pair carries stylish nonleather shoes and boots.

Wilson Sporting Goods Company
8700 W. Bryn Mawr Ave., Chicago, IL 60631
Tel.: 773-714-6400 • E-Mail: info@team.wilsonsports.com
Web site: www.wilsonsports.com
Makes nonleather footballs, etc.

Yak Pak
10 Jay St., Brooklyn, NY 11201
Tel.: 800-2-YAKPAK • E-Mail: admin@yakpak.com
Web site: www.yakpak.com
This company sells many different styles of synthetic bags.
🛒

Companies listed in this guide that are marked with a (🛒) are included in PETA's online shopping mall at wwwPETAMall.com.

Athletic Shoes
Active Soles
Adidas
Asics
Avia
Converse
Etnies
Etonic Shoes
Fila
Keds
New Balance
Nike
Osiris
Payless Shoe Source
Reebok
Road Runner Sports
Saucony
Soap Shoes
Teva
Tretorn

Bags
Aesop
American Hemp and
    Earth Goods
Ecolution
Esprit
Ex-tredz
Heartland Products ⛟
Ohio Hempery Catalog
Pangea ⛟
Payless Shoe Source
Planet Hemp
Timberland
Tomorrow's World
Used Rubber USA
Vegan Wares ⛟

Balls
The OOOF Ball Company

Spalding Sports
V Sports
Wilson Sporting Goods
    Company

Baseball Gloves
Heartland Products ⛟

Belts
Aesop
Ethical Wares ⛟
Ex-tredz
Heartland Products ⛟
NoBull Footwear
Ohio Hempery Catalog
Pangea ⛟
Tomorrow's World
Unlisted by Kenneth Cole
Used Rubber USA
Veganline
Vegan Wares ⛟
Vegetarian Shoes
Yak Pak ⛟

Biking Gloves
REI

Bowling Shoes
Dexter Shoes

Coats & Jackets
Evolutionary Fur
Ex-tredz
Heartland Products ⛟
NoBull Footwear
Pangea ⛟
Planet V ⛟
Vegetarian Shoes

Cycling Shoes
Northwave

Dance Shoes
Capezio
Vegan Wares ⛟

Dress Shoes
Aesop
Daniel Green Company
Ethical Wares ⛟
Kenneth Cole Reaction
Lane Bryant
Life Stride
Madeline Stuart Shoes
Masseys
Naturalizer
Nine West
NoBull Footwear
Pangea ⛟
Payless Shoe Source
Planet V ⛟
Prima Royale Shoes
Roaman's
Sam & Libby
Steve Madden
Unlisted by Kenneth Cole
Veganline
Vegan Wares ⛟
Wild Pair

Faux Fur
Evolutionary Fur
Fabulous Furs
Perfect Image

Hiking and Work Boots
Aesop
Bata Shoe Company
Ethical Wares ⛟
Garmont, USA
Heartland Products ⛟
LaCrosse Boots

Last Resort 🛒
NoBull Footwear
Pangea 🛒
Planet V 🛒
REI
Tomorrow's World
Vegetarian Shoes

Motorcycle Apparel
Aerostitch/Rider Warehouse
Competition Accessories
Dennis Kirk
Ethical Wares

Rock-Climbing Shoes
Five Ten

Skateboarding Shoes
DC Shoes
Emerica
Etnies
Osiris

Snowboarding Boots
Airwalk
Burton Snowboards
Heelside Snowboarding

Snow Boots
Naturalizer
Payless Shoe Source

Tap Shoes
Capezio

Tool Belts
Nailers

Wallets
Aesop
American Hemp and
    Earth Goods
NoBull Footwear
Ohio Hempery
Pangea 🛒
Planet Hemp
Used Rubber USA
Vegan Wares 🛒

Western Style Boots
Heartland Products 🛒

Inclusion in this guide does not imply endorsement by PETA of any of the products. We encourage consumers to SHOP RESPONSIBLY and to question companies about their products and business practices before making any purchase.

Out of Africa into Chains

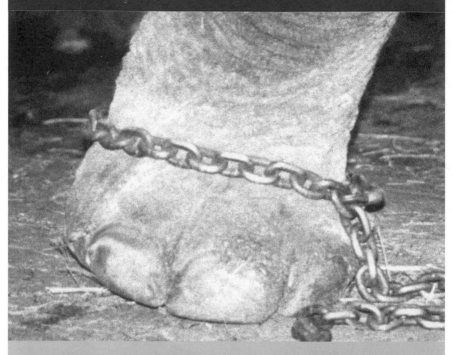

- Elephants spend the majority of their lives shackled or chained, with no exercise or mental stimulation.

- In the wild, elephants spend their entire lives with their families, but circuses separate elephant babies from their mothers as early as age 2 or 3.

- Just recently, a circus had to pay a $20,000 penalty to the government because one of these babies, Kenny, died after the circus forced him to perform while sick.

- "Trainers" torture elephants with bullhooks jabbed into the sensitive skin on their faces and toes and behind their knees to force them to perform, as shown by video footage taken behind the scenes.

BOYCOTT ANIMAL CIRCUSES. YOU CHOOSE. THEY CAN'T.

PeTA PEOPLE FOR THE ETHICAL TREATMENT OF ANIMALS
501 FRONT ST., NORFOLK, VA 23510 • 757-622-PETA • www.Circuses.com

HEALTH CHARITIES: HELPING OR HURTING?

When you donate to a charity, do you know where the money actually goes? Could your gift be contributing to animal suffering?

Some health charities ask for donations to help people with diseases and disabilities yet spend the money to bankroll horrific experiments on dogs, rabbits, rats, mice, primates, hamsters, pigs, ferrets, frogs, fish, guinea pigs, sheep, birds, and other animals. While human health needs cry out for attention and so many people are going without medical care, animal experimentation enriches laboratories and scientists but drains money from relevant and effective projects that could really help save lives.

HEALING WITHOUT HURTING

Instead of ravaging animals' bodies for cures for human diseases, compassionate charities focus their research where the best hope of a breakthrough lies: on humans.

They realize that animal experiments are unnecessary, unreliable, and sometimes dangerously misleading. Enormous variations exist among rats, rabbits, dogs, pigs, and human beings, and meaningful scientific conclusions cannot be drawn about one species by studying another. Non-animal methods provide a more accurate means of testing, and their results can be extrapolated more reliably.

Compassionate, modern charities know that we can improve treatments through up-to-date, non-animal methods, and they fund only non-animal research, leading to real progress in the prevention and treatment of disease—without starving, crippling, burning, poisoning, or cutting open animals.

PEOPLE WHO ARE
VIOLENT
TO ANIMALS
RARELY STOP THERE

Studies show that people who abuse their pets are likely to abuse their kids. So if you see an animal mistreated or neglected, please report it. Because the parent who comes home and kicks the dog is probably just warming up.

PeTA PEOPLE FOR THE ETHICAL TREATMENT OF ANIMALS
501 FRONT ST., NORFOLK, VA 23510 • 757-622-7382 • www.peta-online.org

HEALTH CHARITIES THAT DON'T TEST ON ANIMALS

WHAT TYPES OF CHARITIES ARE ON THE "DON'T TEST" LIST?

Health charities and service organizations that do not conduct or fund experiments on animals are included on the "don't test" list. These organizations deal with human health issues ranging from birth defects to heart disease to substance abuse. Some fund non-animal research to find treatments and cures for diseases and disabilities, while others provide services and direct care to people living with physical or mental ailments.

HOW DOES A CHARITY GET ON THE LIST?

Charities that are listed have signed PETA's statement of assurance certifying that neither they nor their affiliated organizations conduct or fund any experiments on animals and will not do so in the future. Those marked with a check (✓) are presently observing a moratorium on (I.e., current suspension of) animal experiments.

Please contact PETA if you know the address of a charity that is not listed, including local health service organizations. PETA will be happy to inquire about a charity's animal-testing policy, but we also encourage you to inquire yourself, as it is important that charities hear directly from compassionate citizens who are opposed to animal testing.

The following health charities and service organizations **do not** conduct or fund animal experiments. They may deal with several issues, including nonhealth-related issues, but they are listed according to their primary health focus. For more information on the programs and activities of an organization, please contact the organization.

AIDS/HIV

Charlotte HIV/AIDS Network, Inc. (CHAN)
P.O. Box 4229
Port Charlotte, FL 33949-4229
941-625-6650
941-625-AIDS

Chicago House
1925 N. Clayburn, Ste. 401
Chicago, IL 60614
312-248-5200

Children's Immune Disorder
16888 Greenfield Rd.
Detroit, MI 48235-3707
313-837-7800

Concerned Citizens for Humanity
3580 Main St., Ste. 115
Hartford, CT 06120-1121
860-560-0833

Design Industries Foundation Fighting AIDS (DIFFA)
150 W. 26th St., Ste. 602
New York, NY 10001
212-645-0534

Health Cares Exchange Initiative, Inc.
P.O. Box 31
The State House
Boston, MA 02133
617-499-7780

Joshua Tree Feeding Program, Inc.
P.O. Box 7056
Phoenix, AZ 85011-7056
602-264-0223

Loving Arms
P.O. Box 3368
Memphis, TN 38173
901-725-6730

Miracle House
P.O. Box 30931
New York, NY 10011-0109
212-367-9281

Phoenix Shanti Group, Inc.
2020 W. Indian School Rd. #50
Phoenix, AZ 85015
602-279-0008

Puerto Rico Community Network for Clinical Research on AIDS
One Stop Station, #30
P.O. Box 70292
San Juan, PR 00936-8292
809-753-9443

Santa Fe Cares
P.O. Box 1255
Santa Fe, NM 87504-1255
505-989-9255
www.santafecares.org

ARTHRITIS

Arthritis Fund, aka the Rheumatoid Disease Foundation
711 Sweetgum Dr. S.W. #A
Fairview, TN 37062-9384
615-646-1030

BIRTH DEFECTS

Birth Defect Research for Children, Inc.
930 Woodcock Rd.
Ste. 225
Orlando, FL 32803
800-313-2232
www.birthdefects.org

Easter Seals
230 W. Monroe St.
Ste. 1800
Chicago, IL 60606
312-726-6200
www.easter-seals.org

Little People's Research Fund, Inc.
80 Sister Pierre Dr.
Towson, MD 21204
800-232-5773

National Craniofacial Association
P.O. Box 11082
Chattanooga, TN 37401
800-332-2373

Puerto Rico Down Syndrome Foundation
P.O. Box 195273
San Juan, PR 00919-5273
787-268-DOWN

Warner House
1023 E. Chapman Ave.
Fullerton, CA 92831
714-441-2600

BLIND/VISUALLY IMPAIRED

American Association of the Deaf-Blind
814 Thayer Ave., Ste. 302
Silver Spring, MD 20910-4500

Collier County Association for the Blind
4701 Golden Gate Pkwy.
Naples, FL 34116
941-649-1122

Connecticut Institute for the Blind/Oak Hill
120 Holcomb St.
Hartford, CT 06112-1589
860-242-2274

Cumberland County Association for the Blind
837 Robeson St.
Fayetteville, NC 28305
910-483-2719

Deaf-Blind Service Center
2366 Eastlake Ave. E.
Ste. 206
Seattle, WA 98102
206-323-9178

Independence for the Blind,
Inc.
1278 Paul Russell Rd.
Tallahassee, FL 32301
904-942-3658

Living Skills Center for
Visually Impaired
13830-B San Pablo Ave.
San Pablo, CA 94806
510-234-4984

National Federation of the
Blind, Inc.
1800 Johnson St.
Baltimore, MD 21230
410-659-9314

Radio Information Service
2100 Wharton St., Ste. 140
Pittsburgh, PA 15203
412-488-3944

VISIONS/Services for the
Blind and Visually Impaired
500 Greenwich St., 3rd Fl.
New York, NY 10013-1354
888-245-8333
www.visionsvcb.org

Washington Volunteer
Readers for the Blind
901 G St. N.W.
Washington, DC 20001
202-727-2142

BLOOD

Michigan Community
Blood Centers
P.O. 1704
Grand Rapids, MI 49501-1704
800-742-6317

BURNS

Children's Burn Foundation
4929 Van Nuys Blvd.
Sherman Oaks, CA 91403
818-907-2822

CANCER

A.P. John Institute for
Cancer Research
67 Arch St.
Greenwich, CT 06830
203-661-2571

Calvary Fund, Inc.
Calvary Hospital
1740 Eastchester Rd.
Bronx, NY 10461

Cancer Care Services
605 W. Magnolia
Ft. Worth, TX 76104
817-921-0653

Cancer Project
c/o PCRM
5100 Wisconsin Ave. N.W.
Ste. 404
Washington, DC 20016
202-686-2210

Danville Cancer
Association, Inc.
1225 W. Main St.
P.O. Box 2148
Danville, VA 24541
804-792-3700

The Garland Appeal
65 Marathon House
200 Marylebone Rd.
London NW1 5PL England
01728 454820
www.garlandappeal.com

Gilda Radner Familial
Ovarian Cancer Registry
Rosewell Park Cancer
Institute
Elm and Carlton Sts.
Buffalo, NY 14263-0001
716-845-8059

Miracle House
P.O. Box 30931
New York, NY 10011-0109
212-367-9281

National Alliance of Breast
Cancer Organizations
(NABCO)
9 E. 37th St., 10th Fl.
New York, NY 10016
212-889-0606
www.NABCO.org

National Children's Cancer
Society
1015 Locust, Ste. 1040
St. Louis, MO 63101
314-241-1600

Quest Cancer Research
Woodbury, Harlow Rd.
Roydon, Harlow, Essex
CM19 5HF England
01279 792233

Share
1501 Broadway, Ste. 1720
New York, NY 10036
212-719-0364

Skin Cancer Foundation
245 Fifth Ave., Ste. 1403
New York, NY 10016
800-754-6490

Tomorrows Children's Fund
Hackensack University
Medical Center
30 Prospect Ave.
Hackensack, NJ 07601
201-996-5500

CHILDREN

Birth Defect Research for Children, Inc.
930 Woodcock Rd.
Ste. 225
Orlando, FL 32803
800-313-2232
www.birthdefects.org

Children's Burn Foundation
4929 Van Nuys Blvd.
Sherman Oaks, CA 91403
818-907-2822

Children's Diagnostic Center, Inc.
2100 Pleasant Ave.
Hamilton, OH 45015

Children's Immune Disorder
16888 Greenfield Rd.
Detroit, MI 48235-3707
313-837-7800

Children's Wish Foundation International
8615 Roswell Rd.
Atlanta, GA 30350-4867
800-323-WISH

Crestwood Children's Center
2075 Scottsville Rd.
Rochester, NY 14623-2098
716-436-4442

Eagle Valley Children's Home
2300 Eagle Valley Ranch Rd.
Carson City, NV 89703
702-882-1188

Five Acres/The Boys' and Girls' Aid Society of Los Angeles
760 W. Mountain View St.
Altadena, CA 91001
818-798-6793
213-681-4827
www.5acres.org

Help Hospitalized Children's Fund
10723 Preston Rd., #132
Dallas, TX 75230-3806
214-696-4843

Miracle Flights
2756 N. Green Valley Pkwy.
Ste. 115
Green Valley, NV 89014-2100
800-FLY-1711

National Children's Cancer Society
1015 Locust, Ste. 1040
St. Louis, MO 63101
314-241-1600

Pathfinder International
9 Galen St., Ste. 217
Watertown, MA 02172-4501
617-924-7200

Rainbow Kids
P.O. Box 70844
Richmond, VA 23255
804-288-0479

Tomorrows Children's Fund
Hackensack University Medical Center
30 Prospect Ave.
Hackensack, NJ 07601
201-996-5500

DEAF/HEARING-IMPAIRED

Be an Angel Fund
T.H. Rogers School
5840 San Felipe
Houston, TX 77057
713-917-3568

Better Hearing Institute
P.O. Box 1840
Washington, DC 20013
800-EAR-WELL
www.betterhearing.org

Chicago Hearing Society
332 S. Michigan Ave.
Ste. 714
Chicago, IL 60604
312-939-6888
dhhs@lancnews.infi.net

Deaf Action Center
3115 Crestview Dr.
Dallas, TX 75235
214-521-0407

Deaf-Blind Service Center
2366 Eastlake Ave. E.
Ste. 206
Seattle, WA 98102
206-323-9178

Deaf Independent Living Association, Inc.
P.O. Box 4038
Salisbury, MD 21803-4038
410-742-5052

Deaf Service Center of St. John's County
207 San Marco Ave., #38
St. Augustine, FL 32084-2762

Institute for Rehabilitation, Research, and Recreation, Inc.
P.O. Box 1025
Pendleton, OR 97801
541-276-2752

League for the Hard of Hearing
71 W. 23rd St.
New York, NY 10010-4162
212-741-7650
www.lhh.org

Minnesota State Academy
for the Deaf
P.O. Box 308
Faribault, MN 55021
800-657-3996

DISABLED, DEVELOPMENTALLY

Achievements, Inc.
101 Mineral Ave.
Libby, MT 59923
406-293-8848

Adult Activity Services
307 E. Atlantic St.
Emporia, VA 23847
804-634-2124

Adult Training and
Habilitation Center
311 Fairlawn Ave. W.
Box 600
Winsted, MN 55395
612-485-4191

Association for Community
Living
One Carando Dr.
Springfield, MA 01104-3211
413-732-0531

Burnt Mountain Center
P.O. Box 337
Jasper, GA 30143
706-692-6016

Butler Valley, Inc.
380 12th St.
Arcata, CA 95521

Career Development
Center
2110 W. Delaware
Fairfield, IL 62837

Carroll Haven Achieving
New Growth Experiences
(CHANGE)
115 Stoner Ave.
Westminster, MD 21157-5443
410-876-2179

Community Services
452 Delaware Ave.
Buffalo, NY 14202-1515
716-883-8888

Concerned Citizens for the
Developmentally Disabled
P.O. Box 725, 303B
S. Washington St.
Chillicothe, MO 64601
816-646-0109

Creative Employment
Opportunities
50711 Wing Dr.
Shelby Twp., MI 48315
810-566-4770

DeWitt County Human
Resource Center
1150 Rte. 54 W.
Clinton, IL 61727
217-935-9496

Eagle Valley Children's
Home
2300 Eagle Valley Ranch Rd.
Carson City, NV 89703
702-882-1188

EYAS Corporation
411 Scarlet Sage St.
Punta Gorda, FL 33950
813-575-2255

Hartville Meadows
P.O. Box 1055
Hartville, OH 44632
216-877-3694

Hebron Community, Inc.
P.O. Box 11
Lawrenceville, VA 23868

Hope House Foundation
100 W. Plume St., Ste. 224
Norfolk, VA 23510
757-625-6161

Horizons Specialized
Services, Inc.
405 Oak St.
Steamboat Springs, CO
80477-4867
303-879-4466

Kensington Community
Corporation for Individual
Dignity
5425 Oxford Ave.
Philadelphia, PA 19124
215-288-9797

Mountain Valley
Developmental Services
P.O. Box 338
Glenwood Springs, CO
81602
970-945-2306

Mt. Angel Training Center
and Residential Services
P.O. Box 78
Mt. Angel, OR 97362
503-845-9214

New Opportunities
1400 Seventh St.
Madison, IL 62060
618-876-3178

Nia Comprehensive Center
for Developmental
Disabilities
1808 S. State St.
Chicago, IL 60616
312-949-1808
800-NIA-1976

Opportunities for
Handicapped, Inc.
3340 Marysville Blvd.
Sacramento, CA 95838
916-925-3522

Orange County Association
for the Help of Retarded
Citizens
249 Broadway
Newburgh, NY 12550
914-561-0670

Outlook Nashville, Inc.
3004 Tuggle Ave.
Nashville, TN 37211
615-834-7570

Phoenix Services, Inc.
1 Cumberland St.
Lebanon, PA 17042
717-270-1222

Pleasant View Homes, Inc.
P.O. Box 426
Broadway, VA 22815
540-896-8255

Primrose Center
2733 S. Fern Creek Ave.
Orlando, FL 32806-5591
407-898-7201

Project Independence of Queens
169-18 Southside Ave.
2nd Fl.
Jamaica, NY 11432
718-657-1739

RocVale Children's Home
4450 N. Rockton Ave.
Rockford, IL 61103
815-654-3050

San Antonio State School
P.O. Box 14700
San Antonio, TX 78214-0700
210-532-0700

Society to Aid Retarded, Inc. (S.T.A.R.)
P.O. Box 1075
Torrance, CA 90505

Southwest Human Development
202 E. Earll Dr., Ste. 140
Phoenix, AZ 85012
602-266-5976

St. Joseph Home, Inc.
1226 S. Sunbury Rd.
Westerville, OH 43081-9105

Swift County Developmental Achievement Center
2135 Minnesota Ave.
Bldg. 1
Benson, MN 56215
320-843-4201

DISABLED, PHYSICALLY

Access to Independence, Inc.
2345 Atwood Ave.
Madison, WI 53714-1039

A+ Home Care, Inc.
8932 Old Cedar Ave. S.
Bloomington, MN 55425
800-603-7760

Creative Recreation in Special Populations, Inc. (CRISP)
P.O. Box 1086
Fort Collins, CO 80522
970-493-4454

Disabled American Veterans
P.O. Box 14301
Cincinnati, OH 45250-0301
606-441-7300

Dystonia Support System
P.O. Box 21367
Cleveland, OH 44121-0367
216-321-4137

Getabout
P.O. Box 224
New Canaan, CT 06840-0224
203-966-1881

Greener Globe
600 Treese Way
Roseville, CA 95678
916-774-6498

Independence Crossroads
8932 Old Cedar Ave. S.
Bloomington, MN 55425
612-854-8004

Michigan Wheelchair Athletic Association
P.O. Box 1455
Troy, MI 48099
810-979-8253
michwaa@juno.com

Mower Council for the Handicapped
111 N. Main St.
Austin, MN 55912-3404
507-433-9609

San Francisco Committee for Aid of Russian Disabled Veterans
651 11th Ave.
San Francisco, CA 94118-3612

Southwestern Independent Living Center
843 N. Main St.
Jamestown, NY 14701
716-661-3010

Special People, Inc.
Human Resources
City Hall
1420 Miner St.
Des Plaines, IL 60016

United Amputee Services
P.O. Box 4277
Winter Park, FL 32793
407-678-2920
vprice@magicnet.net

DISABLED, PHYSICALLY AND/OR DEVELOPMENTALLY

Alaska Services for Enabling Technology
P.O. Box 6485
Sitka, AK 99835
907-747-7615

Be an Angel Fund
T.H. Rogers School
5840 San Felipe
Houston, TX 77057
713-917-3568

Carroll County Health and Home Care Services
Carroll County Complex
Ossipee, NH 03864
800-499-4171

Comprehensive Advocacy, Inc.
4477 Emerald, Ste. B-100
Boise, ID 83706-2044
800-632-5125

Disability Rights Education & Defense Fund (DREDF)
2212 Sixth St.
Berkeley, CA 94710
510-644-2555

Disabled Resource Services
424 Pine St., Ste. 101
Fort Collins, CO 80524-2421
970-482-2700

Families Helping Families at the Crossroads of Louisiana
818 Main St., Ste. A
Pineville, LA 71360
318-445-7900
800-259-7200

F.A.M.I.L.Y. One-on-One Services
P.O. Box 92
W. Jordan, UT 84084
801-268-6929

Friends of the Handicapped, Inc.
P.O. Box 29
Perkasie, PA 18944
215-257-8732

Heartland Opportunity Center
Madera Center
323 N. E St.
Madera, CA 93638-3245
209-674-8828

Hodan Center, Inc.
941 W. Fountain St.
P.O. Box 212
Mineral Point, WI 53565
608-987-3336

Humboldt Community Access and Resource Center (HCAR)
P.O. Box 2010
Eureka, CA 95502

Indiana Rehabilitation Association
P.O. Box 44174
Indianapolis, IN 46244-0174
317-264-1222

Lifegains, Inc.
1601 S. Sterling St.
P.O. Drawer 1569
Morganton, NC 28680-1569
704-255-8845

Maidstone Foundation, Inc.
1225 Broadway
New York, NY 10001
212-889-5760

Maine Independent Living Services, Inc.
424 Western Ave.
Augusta, ME 04330-6014
800-499-5434

North Country Center for Independence
159 Margaret St., Ste. 202
Plattsburgh, NY 12901
518-563-9058
ncci@slic.com

Open Door, Inc.
1445 S.E. Crystal Lake Dr.
Corvallis, OR 97333
503-752-9724

Options Center for Independent Living
61 Meadowview Ctr.
Kankakee, IL 60901
815-936-0100

Ozarks Valley Community Service, Inc. (OVCS)
135 S. Main
Ironton, MO 63650-0156
573-546-2418

POWERS Coalition
P.O. Box 618
Sterling, VA 20167

Project Independence of Eastern Connecticut
401 W. Thames St.
Unit 1601
Norwich, CT 06360
203-886-0677

Rehabilitation Center
1439 Buffalo St.
Olean, NY 14760
716-372-8909

Resource Center for Accessible Living, Inc.
602 Albany Ave.
Kingston, NY 12401
914-331-0541

Riverfront Foundation
944 Green Bay St.
La Crosse, WI 54601
608-784-9450

Rockingham Opportunities
342 Cherokee Camp Rd.
Reidsville, NC 27320
336-342-4761

Sheltered Workshop
P.O. Box 2002
Clarksburg, WV 26302-2002
304-623-3757

Society for Assisted Living (SAL)
4283 Paradise Rd.
Seville, OH 44273
330-725-7041
330-336-2045

141

Southwest Center for
Independent Living
1856 E. Cinderella
Springfield, MO 65804
800-676-7245

Specialized Training for
Adult Rehabilitation
(START)
20 N. 13th St.
Murphysboro, IL 62966-0938
618-687-2378

Turn Community Services
P.O. Box 1287
Salt Lake City, UT 84110-1287
801-359-8876

Victor C. Neuman
Association
1259 W. Fry St.
Chicago, IL 60622
312-491-1160

Vocational Services, Inc.
(VSI)
115 Blue Jay Dr.
Liberty, MO 64068
816-781-6292

VOLAR Center for
Independent Living
8929 Viscount, Ste. 101
El Paso, TX 79225
915-591-0800
Volar1@whc.net

Waukesha Training Center
300 S. Prairie
Waukesha, WI 53186
414-547-6821

Western Carolina Center
Foundation, Inc.
P.O. Box 646
Morganton, NC 28680-0646
704-433-2862

Windhorse Foundation
1614 Camp Springs Rd.
Reidsville, NC 27320
910-969-9590

Workshop/Northeast
Career Planning
339 Broadway
Menards, NY 12204
518-463-8051

ELDERLY

Aging & Disabled Services,
Inc.
811 S. Palmer Ave.
Box 142
Georgiana, AL 36033

Beth Haven
2500 Pleasant St.
Hannibal, MO 63401
573-221-6000

Carroll County Health and
Home Care Services
Carroll County Complex
Ossipee, NH 03864
800-499-4171

Creative Recreation in
Special Populations, Inc.
(CRISP)
P.O. Box 1086
Fort Collins, CO 80522
970-493-4454

DARTS
1645 Marthaler Ln. W.
St. Paul, MN 55118
612-455-1560

Getabout
P.O. Box 224
New Canaan, CT 06840-0224
203-966-1881

Prairie Mission Retirement
Village
242 Carroll St.
R.R. 1, Box 1Z
St. Paul, KS 66771
316-449-2400

Project Independence of
Eastern Connecticut
401 W. Thames St.
Unit 1601
Norwich, CT 06360
203-886-0677

Wesley Heights
580 Long Hill Ave.
Shelton, CT 06484
203-929-5396

**EMOTIONAL/BEHAVIORAL
DISORDERS**

AIMCenter
1903 McCallie Ave.
Chattanooga, TN 37404
615-624-4800

Burke Foundation
20800 Farm Rd. 150 W.
Driftwood, TX 78619
512-858-4258

Crestwood Children's
Center
2075 Scottsville Rd.
Rochester, NY 14623-2098
716-436-4442

Federation of Families for
Children's Mental Health
1021 Prince St.
Alexandria, VA 22314-2971
703-864-7710
www.ffcmh.org

Lake Whatcom Center
3400 Agate Hts.
Bellingham, WA 98226
360-676-6000

Parents and Children
Coping Together
308 W. Broad St.
Richmond, VA 23220-4219
804-225-0002
800-788-0097

Rimrock Foundation
1231 N. 29th St.
Billings, MT 59101
800-227-3953

Staten Island Mental Health Society, Inc.
669 Castleton Ave.
Staten Island, NY 10301
718-442-2225

Timberlawn Psychiatric Research Foundation, Inc.
P.O. Box 270789
Dallas, TX 75227-0789
214-338-0451

TRANSACT Health Systems of Central Pennsylvania
90 Beaver Dr.
DuBois, PA 15801
814-371-0414

Youth Services for Oklahoma County
21 N.E. 50th St.
Oklahoma City, OK 73105-1811
405-235-7537

HOME CARE/MEALS

Bronx Home Care Services, Inc.
3956 Bronxwood Ave.
Bronx, NY 10466
718-231-6292

Mobile Meals, Inc.
368 S. Main St.
Akron, OH 44311-1014
330-376-7717
800-TLC-MEAL

KIDNEY

American Kidney Fund
6110 Executive Blvd.
Ste. 1010
Rockville, MD 20852
800-638-8299
www.arbon.com/kidney/home.htm
✓

MISCELLANEOUS

American Fund for Alternatives to Animal Research
175 W. 12th St., Ste. 16G
New York, NY 10011-8220
212-989-8073

American Leprosy Missions
1 ALMWay
Greenville, SC 29601
800-543-3135
www.leprosy.org

American Spinal Research Foundation
900 E. Tasman Dr.
San Jose, CA 95134
408-944-6066

American Vitiligo Research Foundation, Inc.
P.O. Box 7540
Clearwater, FL 33758
727-461-3899

Colostomy Society of New York, G.P.O.
Box 517
New York, NY 10016
212-221-1246

Endometriosis Association
8585 N. 76th Pl.
Milwaukee, WI 53223
414-355-2200
✓

Floating Hospital
Pier 11
East River at Wall St.
New York, NY 10005
212-514-7440

Follow-Your-Heart Foundation
P.O. Box 6867
Malibu, CA 90265
818-673-1660
www.followyourheart.org

Greater Erie Eye and Organ Bank, Inc.
5015 Richmond St.
Erie, PA 16509-1949
814-866-3545

MCS Referral and Resources (Multiple Chemical Sensitivity)
508 Westgate Rd.
Baltimore, MD 21229-2343
410-448-3319
donnaya@rtk.net

National Stuttering Project
5100 E. LaPalma Ave.
Ste. 208
Anaheim Hills, CA 92807
714-693-7480
800-364-1677

Seva Foundation
1786 Fifth St.
Berkeley, CA 94710
510-845-7382
www.seva.org

Thyroid Society
7515 S. Main St., Ste. 545
Houston, TX 77030
800-THYROID
www.the-thyroid-society.org

Transplantation Society of Michigan
2203 Platt Rd.
Ann Arbor, MI 48104
800-247-7250

Vulvar Pain Foundation
P.O. Drawer 177
Graham, NC 27253
910-226-0704

PARALYSIS

**Spinal Cord Injury Network
International**
3911 Princeton Dr.
Santa Rosa, CA 95405
800-548-CORD
www.sonic.net/~spinal
spinal@sonic.net

STROKE

**Palm Springs Stroke
Activity Center**
P.O. Box 355
Palm Springs, CA 92263-0355
619-323-7676
PsStrkCntr@aol.com

**Stroke Survivors Support
Group of Pueblo**
710½ E. Mesa Ave.
Pueblo, CO 81006
719-583-8498

SUBSTANCE ABUSE

**Center for Creative
Alternatives**
1700 Adams, Ste. 201
Costa Mesa, CA 92626
714-437-9535

Family Service Association
31 W. Market St.
Wilkes-Barre, PA 18701-1304
717-823-5144

Friendly Hand Foundation
347 S. Normandie Ave.
Los Angeles, CA 90020
213-389-9964

**Highland Waterford Center,
Inc.**
4501 Grange Hall Rd.
Holly, MI 48442
810-634-0140

**Prevention of Alcohol
Problems, Inc.**
2125 Glenhaven Ln. N.
Brooklyn Park, MN 55443-3806
612-729-3047

**Samaritan Recovery
Community, Inc.**
319 S. Fourth St.
Nashville, TN 37206
615-244-4802

TRAUMA/INJURY

**Brain Injury Association of
Florida, Inc.**
201 E. Sample Rd.
Pompano Beach, FL 33064
954-786-2400

Trauma Foundation
San Francisco General
Hospital
Bldg. 1, Rm. 1
1001 Protrero
San Francisco, CA 94110
415-821-8209

VETERANS

**American Veteran's Relief
Fund, Inc.**
5930E Royal Ln.
Dallas, TX 75230-3849
214-696-3784

Help Hospitalized Veterans
36585 Penfield Ln.
Winchester, VA 92596

**San Francisco Committee
for Aid of Russian Disabled
Veterans**
651 11th Ave.
San Francisco, CA 94118-3612

HEALTH CHARITIES THAT TEST ON ANIMALS

WHAT TYPES OF CHARITIES ARE ON THE "DO TEST" LIST?

Health charities that conduct or fund experiments on animals are included on the "do test" list. These organizations deal with human health issues ranging from lung cancer to drug addiction to blindness. While some do have relevant and effective projects that help improve lives, all of them drain money away from these projects in order to support cruel experiments on animals. They starve, cripple, burn, poison, and slice open animals to study human diseases and disabilities. Such experiments are of no practical benefit to anyone. They are unnecessary, unreliable, and sometimes dangerously misleading. "Enormous variations exist among rats, rabbits, dogs, pigs, and human beings, and meaningful scientific conclusions cannot be drawn about one species by studying another," says Neal Barnard, M.D. "Non-animal methods provide a more accurate method of testing and can be interpreted more objectively."

WHAT CAN BE DONE TO STOP CHARITIES FROM EXPERIMENTING ON ANIMALS?

Many charities know that we can improve treatments through modern, non-animal methods, and they fund only non-animal research, leading to real progress in the prevention and treatment of disease. The next time you receive a donation request from a health charity, ask if it funds animal tests. Write now to let charities know that you give **only** to organizations that alleviate suffering, not contribute to it.

Please note that most colleges and universities have laboratories that conduct animal experiments for health and other purposes. If you would like to know if a specific school has an animal laboratory, please contact PETA. For information on the experiments being conducted or to voice your opinion, please contact the school.

The following health charities and service organizations **do** conduct or fund animal experiments. They may deal with several issues, including nonhealth-related issues, but they are listed according to their primary health focus. Listed in parentheses are affiliated organizations that may or may not fund animal experiments. For more information on the programs and activities of an organization, please contact the organization or PETA.

AIDS

American Foundation for AIDS Research (AMFAR)
733 Third Ave., 12th Fl.
New York, NY 10017
800-39-AMFAR

Elizabeth Glaser Pediatric AIDS Foundation
2950 31st St., Ste. 125
Santa Monica, CA 90405
316-314-1459
www.pedaids.org

Pediatric AIDS Foundation
1311 Colorado Ave.
Santa Monica, CA 90404
310-395-9051

ALZHEIMER'S DISEASE

Alzheimer's Association
919 N. Michigan Ave.
Ste. 1000
Chicago, IL 60611-1676
312-335-8700
www.alz.org

Alzheimer's Disease Research
15825 Shady Grove Rd.
Ste. 140
Rockville, MD 20850
800-437-AHAF

ARTHRITIS

Arthritis Foundation
1330 W. Peachtree St.
Atlanta, GA 30309
404-872-7100

BIRTH DEFECTS

March of Dimes Birth Defects Foundation
1275 Mamaroneck Ave.
White Plains, NY 10605
914-997-4504
www.modimes.org

Muscular Dystrophy Association
3300 E. Sunrise Dr.
Tucson, AZ 85718-3208
800-572-1717

Shriners Hospitals for Crippled Children, International Shrine Headquarters
2900 Rocky Point Dr.
Tampa, FL 33607
813-281-0300

United Cerebral Palsy
1660 L St. N.W., Ste. 700
Washington, DC 20036
202-776-0406

BLIND/VISUALLY IMPAIRED

Foundation Fighting Blindness
Executive Plaza One
11350 McCormick Rd.
Ste. 800
Hunt Valley, MD 21031-1014
410-785-1414

Massachusetts Lions Eye Research Fund (Lions Club International Foundation)
118 Allen St.
Hampden, MA 01036
413-566-3756

Research to Prevent Blindness
645 Madison Ave., 21st Fl.
New York, NY 10022-1010
800-621-0026

BLOOD

American Red Cross
430 17th St. N.W.
Washington, DC 20006
202-737-8300

**Leukemia & Lymphoma
Society of America**
600 Third Ave.
New York, NY 10016
212-573-8484
www.leukemia.org

**National Hemophilia
Foundation**
110 Greene St., Ste. 303
New York, NY 10012
212-219-8180

BURNS

**Shriners Burn Institute,
International Shrine
Headquarters**
2900 Rocky Point Dr.
Tampa, FL 33607
813-281-0300

CANCER

American Cancer Society
1599 Clifton Rd. N.E.
Atlanta, GA 30329
404-320-3333
www.cancer.org

**American Institute for
Cancer Research**
1759 R St. N.W.
Washington, DC 20009
202-328-7744

The Breast Cancer Fund
282 Second St., 2nd Fl.
San Francisco, CA 94105
415-543-2979
www.breastcancerfund.org

**The Breast Cancer Research
Foundation**
654 Madison Ave., Ste. 1209
New York, NY 10021
646-497-2600
www.bcrfcure.org

**Cancer Research Foundation
of America**
200 Daingerfield Rd.
Ste. 200
Alexandria, VA 22314
703-836-4412

City of Hope
208 W. Eighth St.
Los Angeles, CA 90014
213-626-4611

The Jimmy Fund
171 Dwight Rd.
Long Meadow, MA 01106
413-567-0651
www.jimmyfund.org

**Leukemia & Lymphoma
Society of America**
600 Third Ave.
New York, NY 10016
212-573-8484
www.leukemia.org

**Memorial Sloan-Kettering
Cancer Center**
1275 York Ave.
New York, NY 10021
212-639-2000

**National Foundation for
Cancer Research**
4600 East-West Hwy.
Ste. 525
Bethesda, MD 20814
800-321-2873

**Nina Hyde Center for Breast
Cancer Research, Lombardi
Cancer Research Center**
3800 Reservoir Rd. N.W.
Washington, DC 20007
202-687-4597

**St. Jude Children's Research
Hospital**
501 St. Jude Pl.
Memphis, TN 38105
901-522-9733
www.stjude.org

**Susan G. Komen Breast
Cancer Foundation**
5005 LBJ Fwy., Ste. 370
Dallas, TX 75244
972-855-1600
800-462-9273
www.komen.org

CHILDREN

**Boys Town National
Research Hospital**
555 N. 30th St.
Omaha, NE 68131
402-498-6511
www.boystown.org

**Elizabeth Glaser Pediatric
AIDS Foundation**
2950 31st St., Ste. 125
Santa Monica, CA 90405
316-314-1459
www.pedaids.org

The Jimmy Fund
171 Dwight Rd.
Long Meadow, MA 01106
413-567-0651
www.jimmyfund.org

**Juvenile Diabetes
Foundation International**
120 Wall St.
New York, NY 10005-4001
800-JDF-CURE
www.jdfcure.com

Pediatric AIDS Foundation
1311 Colorado Ave.
Santa Monica, CA 90404
310-395-9051

**Shriners Hospitals for
Crippled Children,
International Shrine
Headquarters**
2900 Rocky Point Dr.
Tampa, FL 33607
813-281-0300

Society for Pediatric Pathology
6278 Old McLean Village Dr.
McLean, VA 22101
703-556-9222

St. Jude Children's Research Hospital
501 St. Jude Pl.
Memphis, TN 38105
901-522-9733
www.stjude.org

Sudden Infant Death Syndrome Alliance
1314 Bedford Ave.
Ste. 210
Baltimore, MD 21208
800-221-SIDS

DEAF/HEARING-IMPAIRED

Boys Town National Research Hospital
555 N. 30th St.
Omaha, NE 68131
402-498-6511
www.boystown.org

DIABETES

American Diabetes Association
1660 Duke St.
Alexandria, VA 22314
703-549-1500

Joslin Diabetes Center
One Joslin Pl.
Boston, MA 02215
617-732-2400

Juvenile Diabetes Foundation International
120 Wall St.
New York, NY 10005-4001
800-JDF-CURE
www.jdfcure.com

ELDERLY

American Federation for Aging Research
1414 Ave. of the Americas
18th Fl.
New York, NY 10019
212-752-2327

EMOTIONAL/BEHAVIORAL DISORDERS

National Alliance for Research of Schizophrenia and Depression
60 Cutter Mill Rd., Ste. 200
Great Neck, NY 11021
516-829-0091

National Alliance for the Mentally Ill
200 N. Glebe Rd.
Ste. 1015
Arlington, VA 22203-3754
703-524-7600

EPILEPSY

Epilepsy Foundation of America
4351 Garden City Dr.
Ste. 500
Landover, MD 20785
301-459-3700

HEART

American Heart Association
7272 Greenville Ave.
Dallas, TX 75231-4596
214-373-6300
www.americanheart.org

National Heart Foundation
15825 Shady Grove Rd.
Ste. 140
Rockville, MD 20850
800-437-AHAF

KIDNEY

National Kidney Foundation
30 E. 33rd St.
New York, NY 10016
212-889-2210
www.kidney.org

LUNG

American Lung Association
1740 Broadway
New York, NY 10019
212-315-8700
www.lungusa.org

MISCELLANEOUS

American Digestive Health Foundation
7910 Woodmont Ave.
Ste. 700
Bethesda, MD 20814-3015
301-654-2635

American Health Assistance Foundation
15825 Shady Grove Rd.
Ste. 140
Rockville, MD 20850
800-437-2423
www.ahaf.org

American Liver Foundation
75 Maiden Ln., Ste. 603
New York, NY 10038
1-800-465-4837
www.liverfoundation.org

Amyotrophic Lateral Sclerosis Association
21021 Ventura Blvd.
Ste. 321
Woodland Hills, CA 91364
818-340-7500

Crohn's & Colitis Foundation of America
386 Park Ave. S.
New York, NY 10016-8804
800-932-2423
www.ccfa.org

Cystic Fibrosis Foundation
6931 Arlington Rd.
Bethesda, MD 20814
800-FIGHT-CF
www.cff.org

Families of Spinal Muscular Atrophy
P.O. Box 196
Libertyville, IL 60048-0196
800-886-1762
www.fsma.org

Huntington's Disease Society of America
158 W. 29th St., 7th Fl.
New York, NY 10001-5300
212-242-1968
www.hdsa.org

International Foundation for Functional Gastrointestinal Disorders
P.O. Box 17864
Milwaukee, WI 53217
414-964-1799

Lupus Foundation of America
1300 Piccard Dr., Ste. 200
Rockville, MD 20850-4303
800-558-0121

National Headache Foundation
428 W. St. James Pl., 2nd Fl.
Chicago, IL 60614-2750
800-843-2256

National Jewish Medical and Research Center
1400 Jackson St.
Denver, CO 80206
303-388-4461
www.nationaljewish.org

National Multiple Sclerosis Society
733 Third Ave., 6th Fl.
New York, NY 10017-3288
212-986-3240
www.nmss.org

National Osteoporosis Foundation
1232 22nd St. N.W.
Washington, DC 20037-1292
202-223-2226
www.nof.org

National Psoriasis Foundation
6600 S.W. 92nd Ave., Ste. 300
Portland, OR 97223-7195
503-244-7404
www.psoriasis.org

National Vitiligo Foundation
P.O. Box 6337
Tyler, TX 75711
903-531-0074
www.nvfi.org

Tourette Syndrome Association
42-40 Bell Blvd.
Bayside, NY 11361-2820
800-237-0717

PARALYSIS

American Paralysis Foundation
500 Morris Ave.
Springfield, NJ 07081
201-379-2690

Eastern Paralyzed Veterans Association
7 Mill Brook Rd.
Wilton, NH 03086
603-654-5511

Miami Project to Cure Paralysis
P.O. Box 016960, R-48
Miami, FL 33101
305-243-6001

Paralyzed Veterans of America
801 18th St. N.W.
Washington, DC 20006-3715
202-872-1300

PARKINSON'S DISEASE

American Parkinson Disease Association
1250 Hylan Blvd.
Staten Island, NY 10305
800-223-2732
www.apdaparkinson.com

National Parkinson Foundation
1501 N.W. Ninth Ave.
Miami, FL 33136
800-327-4545
www.parkinson.org

Parkinson's Disease Foundation, Inc.
710 W. 168th St.
New York, NY 10032-9982
212-923-4700
www.pdf.org

STROKE

National Stroke Association
96 Inverness Dr. E., Ste. I
Englewood, CO 80112-5112
800-STROKES

VETERANS

Eastern Paralyzed Veterans Association
7 Mill Brook Rd.
Wilton, NH 03086
603-654-5511

Paralyzed Veterans of America
801 18th St. N.W.
Washington, DC 20006-3715
202-872-1300

2001 Shopping Guide for Caring Consumers

Redeemable through company only.

2001 Shopping Guide for Caring Consumers

Redeemable through company only.

2001 Shopping Guide for Caring Consumers

Redeemable through company only.

2001 Shopping Guide for Caring Consumers

Redeemable through company only.

2001 Shopping Guide for Caring Consumers

Redeemable through company only.

2001 Shopping Guide for Caring Consumers

Redeemable through company only.

2001 Shopping Guide for Caring Consumers

Redeemable through company only.

2001 Shopping Guide for Caring Consumers

Redeemable through company only.

**2001 Shopping Guide for
Caring Consumers**

Redeemable
through
company
only.

**2001 Shopping Guide for
Caring Consumers**

Redeemable
through
company
only.

**2001 Shopping Guide for
Caring Consumers**

Redeemable
through
company
only.

**2001 Shopping Guide for
Caring Consumers**

Redeemable
through
company
only.

**2001 Shopping Guide for
Caring Consumers**

Redeemable
through
company
only.

**2001 Shopping Guide for
Caring Consumers**

Redeemable
through
company
only.

**2001 Shopping Guide for
Caring Consumers**

Redeemable
through
company
only.

**2001 Shopping Guide for
Caring Consumers**

Redeemable
through
company
only.

PeTA

2001 Shopping Guide for
Caring Consumers

Redeemable
through
company
only.

PeTA

2001 Shopping Guide for
Caring Consumers

Redeemable
through
company
only.

PeTA

2001 Shopping Guide for
Caring Consumers

Redeemable
through
company
only.

PeTA

2001 Shopping Guide for
Caring Consumers

Redeemable
through
company
only.

PeTA

2001 Shopping Guide for
Caring Consumers

Redeemable
through
company
only.

PeTA

2001 Shopping Guide for
Caring Consumers

Redeemable
through
company
only.

PeTA

2001 Shopping Guide for
Caring Consumers

Redeemable
through
company
only.

PeTA

2001 Shopping Guide for
Caring Consumers

Redeemable
through
company
only.

2001 Shopping Guide for Caring Consumers

Redeemable through company only.

2001 Shopping Guide for Caring Consumers

Redeemable through company only.

2001 Shopping Guide for Caring Consumers

Redeemable through company only.

2001 Shopping Guide for Caring Consumers

Redeemable through company only.

2001 Shopping Guide for Caring Consumers

Redeemable through company only.

2001 Shopping Guide for Caring Consumers

Redeemable through company only.

2001 Shopping Guide for Caring Consumers

Redeemable through company only.

2001 Shopping Guide for Caring Consumers

Redeemable through company only.

WHAT IS PETA?

People for the Ethical Treatment of Animals (PETA) is an international nonprofit organization dedicated to exposing and eliminating all animal abuse. PETA uses public education, litigation, research and investigations, media campaigns, and involvement at the grassroots level to accomplish this goal.

With the help of our dedicated members, PETA persuades major corporations to stop testing products on animals; advocates alternatives to eating animals by promoting a vegetarian diet; and has forced the closure of federally funded animal research facilities because of animal abuse.

To help stop the exploitation and abuse of animals, become a PETA member today.

MEMBERSHIP & DONATION FORM

Enclosed is my contribution to assist your vital work in behalf of all animals.

❑ $16　　❑ $25　　❑ $50　　❑ $100　　❑ Other $ _____

(Annual membership is $16.00. Members receive *The PETA Guide to Compassionate Living* and a subscription to PETA's quarterly newsletter.)

❑ I'm already a PETA member. This is an additional donation.

Name _____

Address _____

City_____ State _____ Zip_____

Complete this form and send with your check to:

PeTA PEOPLE FOR THE ETHICAL TREATMENT OF ANIMALS
501 Front St., Norfolk, VA 23510

Thank you from all of us at PETA.

cguide